CW00552358

R

REBELS is an exciting and innovative new series looking at contemporary rebel groups and their place in global politics. Written by leading experts, and published in conjunction with the Department of Peace Studies at the University of Bradford, the books serve as definitive introductions to the individual organizations, whilst seeking to place them within a broader geographical and political framework. They examine the origins, ideology and future direction of each group, whilst posting such questions as 'When does a "rebel" political movement become a "terrorist" organization?' and 'What are the social-economic drivers behind political violence?' Provocative and original, the series is essential reading for anyone interested in how rebel groups operate today.

The Department of Peace Studies is a world-class centre which since 1973 has developed a unique interdisciplinary research culture. Its mission is to engage in empirical, theoretical and applied research in order to prevent and resolve conflicts and develop peaceful societies; and to provide an enabling environment for international research excellence involving diverse and critical approaches.

The editors of Rebels are Nana K. Poku and Anna Mdee.

ALREADY PUBLISHED

Alex Khasnabish, *Zapatistas: Rebellion from the Grassroots to the Global*

FORTHCOMING

Christina Hellmich, *al-Qaeda: From Global Network to Local Franchise*

Ram Manikkalingam, *Tamil Tigers: Dialogue, Terrorism and Nationalism*

About the Author

GARRY LEECH is an independent journalist and author of numerous books including *Beyond Bogotá: Diary of a Drug War Journalist in Colombia* (Beacon Press, 2009), *The Failure of Global Capitalism: From Cape Breton to Colombia and Beyond* (CBU Press, 2009), and *Crude Interventions: The United States, Oil and the New World (Dis)order* (Zed Books, 2006). He is also a lecturer in the Department of Political Science at Cape Breton University.

THE FARC

The Longest Insurgency

GARRY LEECH

Fernwood Publishing
HALIFAX & WINNIPEG

Department of Peace Studies

Zed Books
LONDON & NEW YORK

The FARC: The Longest Insurgency was first published in 2011

Published in Canada by Fernwood Publishing Ltd,
32 Oceanvista Lane, Black Point, Nova Scotia BOJ 1BO
www.fernwoodpublishing.ca

Published in the rest of the world by Zed Books Ltd,
7 Cynthia Street, London N1 9JF, UK and
Room 400, 175 Fifth Avenue, New York, NY 10010, USA
www.zedbooks.co.uk

Designed and typeset in 11 on 14 Monotype Bulmer
by illuminati, Grosmont, www.illuminatibooks.co.uk
Index by John Barker
Cover designed by www.alice-marwick.co.uk
Printed and bound in Great Britain by CPI
Antony Rowe, Chippenham and Eastbourne

Distributed in the USA exclusively by Palgrave Macmillan, a division
of St Martin's Press, LLC, 175 Fifth Avenue, New York, NY 10010, USA

A catalogue record for this book is available from the British Library
Library of Congress Cataloging in Publication Data available

Library and Archives Canada Cataloguing in Publication
Leech, Garry, 1960–
    The FARC : the longest insurgency / Garry Leech.
Includes bibliographical references.
ISBN 978-1-55266-451-3
    1. Fuerzas Armadas Revolucionarias de Colombia.
2. Insurgency—Colombia.   3. Guerrillas—Colombia.
4. Ideology—Colombia.   5. Colombia—History—1946–1974.
6. Colombia—Politics and government—1974–.   I. Title.
F2279.L43 2011   986.106´34   C2011-902300-8

        ISBN 978 1 84813 491 1 hb (Zed Books)
        ISBN 978 1 84813 492 8 pb (Zed Books)
     ISBN 978 1 55266 451 3 (Fernwood Publishing)

Contents

Acknowledgements

I WOULD LIKE TO THANK Steve Law, Eric Fichtl and Terry Gibbs for their close readings of the manuscript and for their insightful suggestions. I'd also like to thank Terry Gibbs for all her support for my work in Colombia over the years, and for being a part of so many great experiences that I have had in that wonderful country. I would also like to extend my gratitude to my editor Ken Barlow of Zed Books for all his work on this project. Finally, I would like to thank numerous Colombians who must remain anonymous due to the nature of this book and its potential impact on their security. This book would not have been possible without them.

Colombia Timeline, 1948–2010

1948   The assassination of popular Liberal Party dissident Jorge Eliécer
        Gaitán on 9 April ignites a Liberal uprising in Bogotá. The
        uprising spreads throughout the country, igniting a decade-long
        civil war between Liberals and Conservatives known simply as
        La Violencia, or The Violence, in which more than 200,000 are
        killed.

1950–53 The Liberal Party boycotts elections that bring hard-line Con-
        servative Party candidate Laureano Gómez to power. The Gómez
        administration launches a reign of terror against Liberal and
        communist insurgents and their sympathizers.

1953–57 Military coup overthrows the Gómez government and General
        Gustavo Rojas Pinilla seizes power. Rojas Pinilla implements
        major public works projects to win support while simultane-
        ously repressing all protest against his dictatorship. Colombian
        Communist Party member Manuel Marulanda organizes armed
        peasant groups in the department of Tolima.

1957   Liberal and Conservative party elites sign a power-sharing agree-
        ment and support public protests and a military coup that
        overthrows Rojas Pinilla.

1958   The National Front government assumes power under the
        power-sharing agreement that calls for the Liberal Party and
        Conservative Party to alternate the presidency every four years

and to split evenly all government posts. The National Front would last until 1974.

1958–64   The level of violence diminishes under the National Front as partisan conflict is replaced by government repression against communist peasants.

1964   Government forces attack the rural community of Marquetalia in Tolima on 27 May. Forty-eight armed peasants led by Manuel Marulanda survive the attack and form a guerrilla movement called the Southern Bloc. They formulate the Agrarian Reform Programme of the Guerrillas at the First Guerrilla Conference on 20 July. The National Liberation Army (ELN) guerrilla group is formed by Cuban-influenced urban intellectuals.

1966   At the Second Guerrilla Conference, the Southern Bloc changes its name to the Revolutionary Armed Forces of Colombia (FARC) and takes the 27 May 1964 attack on Marquetalia as the official date of the founding of the guerrilla organization. The Third and Fourth Conferences of the FARC were held.

1972   The M-19 guerrilla group is formed in opposition to the National Front regime.

1974   The Fifth Conference of the FARC is held. The National Front comes to an end as the Liberal and Conservative Parties field candidates against each other. However, government posts remain evenly divided between the two parties.

1978   The Sixth Conference of the FARC is held and the guerrilla group's chain of command is restructured to account for the growing number of fronts situated throughout the country.

1978–82   The Liberal government of Julio César Turbay Ayala intensifies repression against the expanding guerrilla movements. Cocaine traffickers becoming increasingly powerful economically and politically and, along with large landowners and the Colombian military, begin forming right-wing paramilitary groups to combat the growing strength of the guerrillas.

1982   The Seventh Conference of the FARC is held, in which the guerrilla group changes its name to the Revolutionary Armed Forces of Colombia – People's Army (FARC–EP) and adjusts it military strategy to begin conducting more offensive operations.

1984–85   The Conservative government of Belisario Betancur reaches a ceasefire agreement with the FARC and engages in peace talks. The FARC, the Colombian Communist Party and other leftists form the Patriotic Union (UP) party to participate in elections. Paramilitaries intensify their dirty war against leftists and assassinate more than two thousand members of the UP, including two presidential candidates and four elected congressional representatives, over the next five years.

1985   M-19 guerrillas take over the Palace of Justice, which houses Colombia's Supreme Court. The army kills more than one hundred people, including eleven Supreme Court justices in its two-day offensive to retake the building.

1987   Colombia's various guerrilla groups, including the FARC, form a coalition called the Simón Bolívar Guerrilla Coordinating Committee (CGSB).

1990   On 10 August, the FARC's political leader and secretariat member Jacobo Arenas dies from cancer and is replaced by Alfonso Cano. Liberal President César Gaviria begins implementing neoliberal, or so-called free-market, economic reforms in return for increased military and drug war aid from the United States. In December, the military launches a surprise attack against Casa Verde, the headquarters of the FARC. The M-19 demobilizes and forms a political party called the M-19 Democratic Alliance, which wins a majority of seats in the Constituent Assembly responsible for drafting a new constitution.

1991   In June and September, exploratory talks between the Colombian government and the CGSB, which now consists only of the FARC and ELN, take place in Caracas, Venezuela. The new Colombian Constitution is promulgated in July.

1992   In March, exploratory talks between the Colombian government and the CGSB are renewed in Tlaxcala, México. The talks eventually break down and the CGSB is disbanded.

1993   The Eighth Conference of the FARC is held.

1994   Liberal President Ernesto Samper assumes office. Relations with the United States deteriorate during his four-year term due to accusations that his campaign was funded by the Cali cocaine cartel.

1996   On 30 August, the FARC launches its first large full-frontal as-
        sault on a military base when more than 500 guerrillas kill 54
        soldiers in the battle to capture the Las Delicias army base in
        Putumayo in southern Colombia. The guerrilla group's military
        strength continues to increase dramatically and several more
        successful large-scale assaults against military bases occur in the
        ensuing years.

1997   Regional paramilitary groups form a national organization called
        the United Self-Defense Forces of Colombia (AUC) and ex-
        pand their dirty war to FARC-dominated southern and eastern
        Colombia.

1998   The US Defense Intelligence Agency warns that the FARC could
        defeat the Colombian army within five years. In November, newly
        elected Conservative President Andrés Pastrana withdraws two
        thousand soldiers and police from five municipalities in southern
        Colombia and turns the zone over to the FARC as a safe haven
        in which to conduct peace talks. However, there is no ceasefire
        agreement during the peace process and the war continues to
        rage throughout the rest of the country.

2000   US President Bill Clinton announces a new multibillion-dollar
        counter-narcotics initiative called Plan Colombia. The massive
        increase in military funding makes Colombia the third-largest
        recipient of US aid behind Israel and Egypt. In December,
        Plan Colombia is launched in the southern department of Pu-
        tumayo and in the ensuing years spreads throughout much of
        Colombia.

2002   In February, the peace process ends when President Pastrana
        orders the military to invade the FARC-controlled safe haven.
        The government blames the FARC for its refusal to agree to a
        ceasefire, while the guerrillas point to the government's unwill-
        ingness to seriously negotiate the country's economic and social
        problems and its failure to dismantle the paramilitary groups. In
        July, the Bush administration begins providing counter-terrorism
        funding to the Colombian government as part of the US war on
        terror. In August, newly elected independent President Alvaro
        Uribe assumes office after conducting a hard-line anti-guerrilla

campaign and immediately orders the military to take the offensive against the FARC.

2003   In December, the AUC and the government begin negotiations to establish the terms under which paramilitary fighters would demobilize. Meanwhile, state security forces become more directly involved in the dirty war against leftists through extrajudicial executions, arbitrary arrests, forced displacements and disappearances.

2004   FARC commander Simón Trinidad is captured in Ecuador while trying to contact UN officials in an effort to organize a prisoner exchange between the guerrilla group and the Colombian government. He is returned to Colombia and then extradited to the United States to stand trial on kidnapping and drug-trafficking charges. Trinidad is the highest-ranking FARC member ever to be captured.

2005   The Colombian Congress amends the constitution to allow President Uribe to run for re-election.

2006   President Uribe is re-elected in May. Colombia's attorney general's office uncovers evidence of extensive collusion between paramilitaries, government officials, military officers and multinational corporations in what becomes known as the para-politics scandal. On 22 November, the US and Colombian governments sign a free-trade agreement.

2007   In May, the Ninth Conference of the FARC is held. In response to the para-politics scandal and human rights abuses against Colombian unionists, Democrats in the US Congress block ratification of the free-trade agreement signed by the Bush and Uribe administrations.

2008   On 1 March, the Colombian military finally succeeds in its efforts to kill a member of the FARC's secretariat when it launches a cross-border airstrike into Ecuador that results in the death of the guerrilla group's number two commander Raúl Reyes. Six days later, it is revealed that another secretariat member, Iván Ríos, had been killed by his security chief. And on 26 March, long-time FARC leader Manuel Marulanda dies of a heart attack. Secretariat member Alfonso Cano replaces Marulanda as the FARC's commander-in-chief. In July, the Colombian military rescues fifteen high-profile captives held by the FARC, including former presidential candidate Ingrid Betancourt and three US military contractors who were captured after their plane crashed in southern Colombia.

2009   The Colombian military continues to have success on the battle-field as the FARC presence in many northern regions is virtually eradicated and the guerrilla group is forced to retreat deep into its traditional strongholds in eastern and southern Colombia and in the south-central highlands. The Colombian military also kills and captures several mid-level FARC commanders. In October, the Colombian and US governments sign an agreement that provides the US military with access to seven Colombian military bases for the next ten years. The Colombian Constitutional Court later stalls implementation of the agreement.

2010   In August, Uribe's former minister of defence, Juan Manuel Santos, becomes president. In September, a bombing raid by the Colombian military kills FARC secretariat member Mono Jojoy. Despite enduring military setbacks in recent years, a smaller and more mobile FARC utilizes traditional hit-and-run guerrilla tactics and landmines to kill more than 1,800 soldiers and police in 2010, more than at the height of the conflict in 2002.

200 KM

100 MI

Barranquilla

LA
GUAJIRA

Cartagena

MAGDALENA

CESAR

PANAMA

SUCRE

NORTE DE
SANTANDER

VENEZUELA

CORDOBA

BOLIVAR

Medellín

SANTANDER

ARAUCA

CHOCÓ

CASANARE

CUNDINAMARCA

VICHADA

Bogotá

VALLE DE
CAUCA

TOLIMA

Marquetalia

COLOMBIA

META

GUAINÍA

Cali

HUILA

CAUCA

GUAVIARE

San Vicente
del Caguán

NARIÑO

PUTUMAYO

CAQUETÁ

VAUPÉS

BRAZIL

ECUADOR

AMAZONAS

PERU

Map of Colombia

For Terry, my revolutionary conscience

Introduction

SOMEONE ONCE TOLD ME that Colombia is a lot like Narnia, that mythical paradise created by C.S. Lewis in his fantasy novels for children. Narnia is a magical land of spectacular mountains, forests and oceans; a place where even animals can talk. It is easy to see that sort of magic and fantasy in Colombia. It is a spectacularly beautiful country that is the second most biologically diverse in the world. Furthermore, Colombia gave us Gabriel García Márquez, arguably the most famous author of the literary genre known as magical realism in which the daily realities of life are frequently infused with magical and mystical occurrences. Colombians are fully aware of the beautiful and magical qualities of the country in which they live. In fact, according to a joke that Colombians love to share, when God created the world he paid special attention to Colombia. He was instructing the archangels how to distribute things when, after a while, the archangels began to question God's decisions.

'Divine Master', they said. 'Are you sure you want to give Colombia coasts on two seas, the Pacific and the Caribbean?'

'Yes, I'm sure', He answered resolutely.

'Are you sure you want to give Colombia three major mountain ranges?'

'Yes, I'm sure', He continued.

'Are you sure you want to give so many species of birds and so many emeralds and other natural resources to just one country?' they pleaded.

'Yes, I'm sure', God replied again, this time with a wry smile on His face.

'But is that fair to the rest of the world?' protested the archangels.

'Just do as I say!' God commanded. 'And as for being fair, just wait and see the politicians that I'm going to give them!'

And, as many Colombians are also fully aware, it has been the country's political leaders that lie at the root of the problems that the country has endured since achieving independence two hundred years ago. Colombia's ruling elites have created the conditions that led to the formation of numerous armed insurgencies in recent decades as the marginalized have sought to change the country's traditionally repressive political, social and economic structures. The most prominent contemporary armed insurgency is the Revolutionary Armed Forces of Colombia – People's Army, known by its Spanish-language acronym as the FARC–EP (Fuerzas Armadas Revolucionarias de Colombia – Ejército del Pueblo), or FARC for short.

The FARC is the world's oldest insurgency, having been fighting in the jungles and mountains of Colombia for almost half a century. It is a Marxist–Leninist revolutionary organization and the largest insurgency in Latin America, actually growing in size and military strength in the decade following the end of the Cold War. During that time, it controlled large swaths of rural Colombia, particularly in eastern and southern parts of the country. Largely demonized by Western governments and media, little is actually known about the inner workings of this guerrilla group.

The FARC: The Longest Insurgency begins by examining the roots of the FARC, looking at the context in which the rebel group was formed and its early years. Chapter 2 examines the FARC's political project, particularly its role in the Patriotic Union (Unión Patriótica, UP) political party during the 1980s. The next chapter analyses the rebel group's social and economic policies in communities in its traditional rural strongholds and looks at the issues that lead peasants to join the FARC and their life in the guerrilla group. Chapter 4 examines the FARC's evolving role in the illicit drug trade and the impacts of this on its ideology. The book then looks at how, following 9/11, US policy shifted from viewing the FARC as 'narco-guerrillas' to perceiving them as 'narco-terrorists', and at the security policies of the government of President Alvaro Uribe. Chapter 6 examines Colombia's dire human rights crisis and contextualizes the FARC's violations of international humanitarian law. The book concludes by looking at the future of the FARC, the repeated claims of its imminent demise and the viability of armed struggle in the twenty-first century.

The book draws upon extensive field research conducted in FARC-controlled regions over the past decade, as well as on other texts about Colombia's conflict, Colombian and international news sources, and governmental and non-governmental reports. Ultimately, this book seeks to move beyond the propaganda that dominates so many discussions about the FARC by examining the rebel group's origins, aims and ideology, as well as the reality of armed struggle in rural Colombia.

CHAPTER 1

The Roots of the FARC

IN ORDER to understand the FARC – its longevity as well as its successes and failures – it is important to recognize the historical context out of which this guerrilla group emerged. While Colombia's history resembles that of other Latin American nations in many ways, there are some unique aspects to the country that have impacted it politically, socially and economically. For instance, unlike in any other Latin American country, Colombia's principal cities – Bogotá, Medellín, Cali and Baranquilla – are separated from each other by vast expanses of towering mountain peaks and dense, lowland tropical jungles. Many of Colombia's provincial regions developed in relative isolation from the capital, Bogotá. Prior to the twentieth century, it took less time to travel from the Caribbean port city of Cartagena across the Atlantic Ocean to Paris than to the nation's capital – seated on a savannah 8,600 feet up in the Andes mountains. Those rare occasions on which rural Colombians had to deal with the national government usually involved confrontations with military forces operating in the interests of Bogotá's political and economic elite. This geographic isolation for many Colombians bred a distrust of central government that still persists in rural Colombia. To this day, despite frequent claims made by mainstream analysts that Colombia is Latin America's oldest democracy, the government in Bogotá has never effectively controlled all of the national territory.

Following independence from Spain in 1810, local landed elites, primarily white descendants of Spanish colonial rulers, held political and economic sway throughout Colombia and retained control of the country's prime agricultural land. In essence, independence merely transferred rule from Spanish colonial administrators to an oligarchy comprising Spanish-descended Colombians serving their own political and economic interests. By the mid-nineteenth century, Colombia's new ruling elite had formed two political parties – the Liberals and Conservatives – which would dominate Colombian politics until the end of the twentieth century. Initially, the Liberals favoured a federalist system of government, separation of church and state, and laissez-faire economics, while the Conservatives preferred a strong central government, close ties between church and state, and a government actively involved in economic policymaking. But by the mid-twentieth century, there was little difference between the two parties, particularly regarding economic policy.

Despite the country's formidable geographic barriers, the two parties eventually managed to infiltrate many of Colombia's settled regions, although constituents usually displayed a greater allegiance to regional party officials than to national leaders. Political differences between the Liberal and Conservative elite, both locally and nationally, frequently resulted in outbreaks of violence, pitting party loyalists from each faction against each other. While peasants routinely took part in Colombia's many civil wars, these conflicts were fundamentally between the interests of the ruling elites and were not class-based liberation struggles. Peasants often fought to protect the interests of their

Liberal or Conservative *patrón*, or local landowner, in return for moderate reforms that improved their own lot in life.[1]

The turbulence of the nineteenth century culminated with the War of the Thousand Days (1899–1902). With Colombia's economy suffering from a decline in world coffee prices and Conservatives having held power since 1886, Liberals disputed the 1898 election that brought Conservative candidate Manuel A. Sanclamente to power, and took up arms against the government. The war proved to be the bloodiest of Colombia's many civil conflicts, with as many as 100,000 killed. By the end of 1902, the country's economy was virtually paralysed and government forces held the military advantage, causing the Liberals to agree to lay down their arms in return for amnesty.

The same year saw the Conservative government agree to the Hay–Herrán Treaty that gave the United States the rights to build a transoceanic canal across the Colombian province of Panama. But in 1903, the Colombian Senate unanimously refused to ratify the treaty on the grounds that US control over the canal was incompatible with Colombian sovereignty. In November of that year, Washington was presented with another opportunity to obtain the rights to build the canal when Panamanian secessionists revolted against Bogotá. President Theodore Roosevelt responded to the uprising on the isthmus by dispatching US warships and troops to prevent Colombian forces sent to quell the revolt from reaching Panama City.

Three days later Washington officially recognized Panamanian independence and signed a new treaty with Philip Buneau-Varilla – the former chief engineer of the Panama Canal Company – before legitimate representatives of the new Panamanian government could reach Washington. Roosevelt ignored Panama's protests over plans to establish a canal zone that would effectively cut the new country in half. Colombia also lodged official protests with

Washington for supporting Panamanian independence, but was powerless to do anything about the situation.

While the loss of Panama caused many Colombians to resent and distrust the United States, some of the country's economic elite continued to push for expanded ties with their powerful northern neighbour. Political tensions were partially alleviated in 1922 when the US Senate ratified the Urrutia–Thompson Treaty that called for Washington to pay a $25 million indemnity to Colombia for the US role in Panama's secession.

The ensuing years became known as the 'Dance of the Millions', partly due to the $25 million payment, but primarily because Colombia's coffee production expanded dramatically and its banana, petroleum and manufacturing sectors experienced significant growth. But the huge majority of Colombians were not benefiting from the country's booming economy, and rural and urban workers, often organized by the Colombian Communist Party (Partido Comunista Colombiano, PCC), began demanding social and economic reforms.

The Violence

In the late 1920s, the emergence on the political scene of Jorge Eliécer Gaitán, a dissident Liberal Party member, offered hope to millions of impoverished and downtrodden Colombians. Gaitán first gained prominence with his public denunciations of the Conservative government's role in the Colombian army's 1928 massacre of striking banana workers in the northern town of Ciénaga, accusing the government and the army of being in the pocket of the Boston-based United Fruit Company. Gaitán was also instrumental in the labour and agrarian reform movements that resulted in the introduction of Colombia's first modern agrarian reform law in 1936.[2]

Gaitán's populist rhetoric gained him a substantial following and, by the late 1940s, following a short stint as mayor of Bogotá, he was the presumed favourite to win the 1950 presidential election. Meanwhile, in 1946, the newly elected Conservative government began using violence to reverse some of the moderate reforms that had been implemented by reform-minded Liberals over the previous sixteen years. On 9 April 1948, however, the low-intensity violence exploded when Gaitán was assassinated on a Bogotá street. The Liberal leader's death triggered the Bogotazo, a popular uprising by the Liberal lower classes that resulted in massive destruction and looting in the capital.

Many US officials, including Secretary of State George C. Marshall, who was attending the Ninth International Conference of American States in Bogotá when the violence broke out, believed the Bogotazo was a communist conspiracy to undermine the conference. According to Robert W. Drexler, who served as a US diplomat in Colombia during the 1950s and again in the 1970s,

> The rapidly growing obsession of the United States government with the Communist threat to Latin America can be dated from the Bogotazo, and it was a cruel irony of fate for Colombia that riots there arising from grave social ills led the United States to adopt militaristic anti-Communist policies in the area which generally ignored and sometimes even worsened those domestic problems.[3]

The rioting in Bogotá led to Liberal uprisings throughout the country in what became known as La Violencia, or The Violence. Fearing that the violence might coalesce into a peasant-based social revolution, the national Liberal leadership backed the bloody repression used by the Conservative government to quell it. Despite this loose alliance between the two parties, alleged Conservatives assassinated two high-ranking Liberals in 1949. The Liberal Party responded by boycotting the 1950 presidential election, which was won uncontested by Conservative candidate Laureano Gómez.

Although rebellion had been effectively suppressed in Bogotá, armed peasant uprisings continued throughout the countryside. The increasingly authoritarian Gómez regime – supported by the Catholic Church, a popular target of rebellious Liberal peasants during the uprisings due to its traditional alliance with the Conservatives – elevated the military crackdown to new heights, which only further fuelled the violence. The chaotic conflict included battles not only between Liberal and Conservative peasants, but also between the oligarchy and land-starved peasants, leading many large landowners to abandon their properties for the relative safety of the cities. The United States viewed the Colombian Communist Party's support for the peasants through a Cold War lens and rushed weapons and training to the Colombian military. Close military cooperation between the two countries had already been established when Colombia became the only Latin American country to send combat troops to aid the US war effort in Korea.

In 1952, a 23-year-old Argentine doctor named Ernesto 'Che' Guevara arrived in Colombia after travelling throughout much of South America. During his brief stay, the man who would later inspire many Colombian revolutionaries noted, 'There is more repression of individual freedom here than in any other country we've been to... The atmosphere is tense and a revolution may be brewing.'[4] High-ranking military officials also recognized the possible political and social implications of the rural violence and the inability of Gómez to quell it. And so, in 1953, the Conservative president was ousted by a military coup that brought General Gustavo Rojas Pinilla to power.

Rojas Pinilla, the former commander of a Colombian infantry battalion in Korea, issued an amnesty to all armed peasants in an attempt to bring an end to La Violencia. Many armed Liberal peasants accepted the offer. But shortly afterwards, the government began targeting demobilized Liberal guerrillas. And then, in 1954, Rojas Pinilla launched a major military offensive against communist peasants who had refused to lay down their arms, particularly those in the Villarica region of central Colombia. Thousands of peasants were displaced by the military offensive and, once resettled elsewhere, began forming self-defence groups at the urging of the Colombian Communist Party. The self-defence groups sought to protect themselves from the actions of both the military and large landowners who sought the newly settled lands in the peasant enclaves, or what some analysts have labelled 'independent republics'.

Meanwhile, the Conservative and Liberal elite, concerned about Rojas Pinilla's desire to retain power, organized widespread street protests that toppled the dictator. The two parties then implemented a power-sharing agreement called the National Front. Beginning in 1958, the Conservative and Liberal parties alternated four-year terms in the presidency and divided all government positions evenly between themselves. The National Front marked the end of the factional sparring between elites that had characterized Colombia's political violence from the nineteenth century through La Violencia; however, the new unity government had to contend with armed communist peasants that still sought to address the gross social inequalities so prevalent in Colombia.

The Role of the Communist Party

During the 1930s, the Colombian Communist Party (PCC) had proven effective at organizing – and politicizing – peasants in rural central Colombia, particularly in the department, or province, of Tolima and the south-western part of the department of

Cundinamarca. Unlike most other communist parties in Latin America at the time, the PCC made organizing the rural population a priority. Not surprisingly then, during La Violencia, it was the armed communist peasants in Tolima and surrounding regions that posed the greatest threat to the hegemony of the Conservative and Liberal elite. Most armed Liberal peasants, who, like their communist counterparts, had taken up arms to defend themselves against the repressive actions of the Conservative government in the early years of La Violencia, remained loyal to the Liberal elites following the formation of the National Front government.

The PCC was instrumental in organizing the peasant self-defence movement. The peasant leaders of many of the armed groups were members of the PCC, including Pedro Antonio Marín in Tolima, who would later change his name to Manuel Marulanda Vélez and become the supreme commander of the FARC. Marulanda had grown up in a traditional Liberal family in the department of Quindío in central Colombia, but in his teen years he became a Marxist–Leninist. He began working with the PCC in the late 1940s and became a member in 1952 at the age of 24. Eight years later, Marulanda was elected to the PCC's Central Committee.

During the 1950s, Marulanda was a leading organizer for the PCC in Tolima, becoming instrumental in the establishment of armed peasant groups that sought to defend communities from government repression. According to Marulanda,

> The resistance groups went through the logical and natural process of formation, strengthening and consolidation. It was a process of the emergence of a form of struggle that had no immediate predecessor, rising spontaneously, imprecisely, in which the peasants themselves were protagonists of their own history.[5]

In the enclaves, the communist peasants sought to establish alternative political, social and economic structures to the capitalist model imposed on the rural population by the country's dominant political parties. By the early 1950s, notes historian Gonzalo Sánchez, the communist revolutionaries 'regulated the use of expropriations and the proceeds from them, subordinating individual appetites to the collective good of the resistance.... In some regions of greatest control, production and distribution priorities were set for the civilian population.'[6] According to the FARC's telling of its origins, both the PCC and the leaders of the self-defence groups

> encouraged the peasant communities to share the land among the residents and created mechanisms for collective work and assistance to the individual exploitation of parcels of land and applied the movement's justice by collective decision of assemblies of the populace. These became areas with a new mentality and social and political proposals different from those offered by the regime. The decisive factor was the presence in power of the people themselves.[7]

Father Camilo Torres, Colombia's famous revolutionary priest and one of the early proponents of liberation theology, also acknowledged the escalating level of organizing by the armed peasants:

> Among the peasants, the emergence of violence creates circumstances which force them to abandon their individualism. Joint migrations, defense of the rural communities, organization of production, etc., encouraged a mentality of co-operation, initiative, and class consciousness. A new situation has transformed Colombian rural communities into social units with internal cohesion, initiative, and their own dynamics.[8]

And while there are differing accounts regarding the degree to which peasants succeeded in establishing collective political, social and economic projects, it is clear that the very existence of these radicalized communities posed a threat to the country's ruling elite. This threat led to a shift in the nature of the conflict during the second half of La Violencia, away from a sectarian struggle along party lines to one along class lines. As Torres noted, La Violencia

> started a social process that the ruling classes did not foresee. It has awakened the class consciousness of the peasant, given him group solidarity and a feeling of superiority and confidence to act.... This will have the effect of constituting a social pressure group – economically and even politically capable of changing the social structure in the way least expected and least desired by the ruling class. It is very possible that, due to violence, political sectarianism will be changed into class sectarianism, as has already occurred in many rural areas.[9]

The Rojas Pinilla government responded to the emerging class conflict by banning the PCC and launching military offensives against the peasant enclaves. The US-backed military offensives initially targeted the Sumapaz region just south of Bogotá, forcibly displacing peasants from their homes and lands. These displaced peasants would resettle in the eastern departments of Meta and Caquetá as well as in southern Tolima. These regions would later become the traditional strongholds of the FARC.[10]

In response to the government's offensive, the PCC engaged in a delicate, and contradictory, balancing act with regard to its relations to the armed peasants and the Soviet Union. In 1956, a resolution passed at the Twentieth Congress of the Communist Party of the Soviet Union had called on its party affiliates around the world to seek a non-violent road to revolution. As a result, the PCC publicly denounced the armed struggle being waged by peasants, while covertly supporting the self-defence groups in the countryside.[11] In 1961, however, at its Ninth Congress, the PCC adopted the call for various forms of struggle, including armed struggle.

Operation Marquetalia

By the early 1960s, and in light of the revolution in Cuba, the United States and Colombia's ruling elites sought to ensure that the peasant enclaves were eradicated once and for all. In February 1962, a team from the Special Warfare Center at Fort Bragg, headed by Brigadier General William P. Yarborough, visited Colombia to evaluate the internal security situation and the Colombian army's counter-insurgency strategies. The team's final report recommended that Colombia develop the military and civilian structures necessary to engage in the 'clandestine execution of plans developed by the United States Government toward defined objectives in the political, economic, and military fields', including undertaking 'paramilitary, sabotage and/or terrorist activities against known communist proponents. It should be backed by the United States'.[12]

The report's recommendations were incorporated into the Latin American Security Operation, known as Plan LASO, a US-backed initiative to combat the growing communist influence in Colombia. Utilizing aircraft and weaponry supplied by the United States, the Colombian military intensified its targeting of the peasant enclaves. On 27 May 1964, the Colombian military launched Operation Marquetalia, utilizing 16,000 Colombian troops supported by US-supplied B-26 bombers, to target the small village of the same name. There were forty-eight armed peasant guerrillas in Marquetalia commanded by Marulanda, who had earned the nickname 'Sureshot' due to his sharpshooting prowess, and another member of the PCC named Jacobo Arenas, who would later become the political leader of the FARC. Despite the massive offensive launched against them, all forty-eight guerrillas managed to evade capture or death. Furthermore, in the midst of the offensive, a public assembly was held on 20 July in which the participating peasants approved utilizing a guerrilla strategy and formulated an agrarian reform programme.

The following year, the First Guerrilla Conference took place and the armed peasants from Marquetalia joined with groups from other enclaves and formed the Southern Bloc (Bloqué Sur). They also became mobile and, along with their families and others, expanded their sphere of operations from the Andean highlands in central Colombia to the Amazon rainforest in the eastern part of the country, primarily in the departments of Meta and Caquetá. The peasants colonized the region by establishing small farms, while the Southern Bloc defended the communities from both the military and the encroachment of large landowners who sought to expropriate their new landholdings. Father Torres, who would later join the leftist National Liberation Army (Ejército de Liberación Nacional, ELN) guerrilla group and be killed in his first combat experience, highlighted the organic and radicalizing nature of the relationship between the peasants and the guerrillas:

> Through the guerrillas the rural communities have become integrated within a process of urbanization, with the full range of implications: division of labor, specialization, socio-cultural contact with other groups, socialization, a mental orientation toward change, awakening of social expectations, and the use of methods of action to realize social mobility through channels which the power structure had not foreseen. Furthermore, violence has established the systems necessary for the establishment of a rural sub-culture, a peasant social class, and a revolutionary pressure group constituted by this same class.[13]

In 1966, the Second Guerrilla Conference was convened and the armed peasant groups belonging to the Southern Bloc officially became the FARC, although the guerrilla group considers 27 May 1964, the date of the launching of Operation Marquetalia, to be its actual date of origin. At the second conference, according to the FARC:

> A new national military plan and a more ambitious plan for mass organization, education, publicity and finances were produced.... For the first time it was stated that the FARC guerrilla movement was setting out on a prolonged struggle to take power in unity with the working class and all working people.... It was established clearly that the tactic of mobile guerrilla warfare was adequate and just but that it was necessary to extend activity to new areas of the country.[14]

And so the peasant self-defence groups were transformed into a revolutionary guerrilla force that sought to expand operations throughout the country in order to overthrow the government. According to Marulanda, 'We were building a new type of general staff as the supreme political and military authority, taking care that militarism did not overwhelm everything.'[15] He went on to note that it was vital that the guerrillas were not only trained militarily, but that they were also educated politically and that it was crucial they responded respectfully to the fundamental demands of the peasantry. Perhaps one of the most essential components of surviving as a guerrilla force is the ability to self-analyse. As Marulanda stated, 'We maintain a critical and self-critical attitude in the face of our own political and military errors', which led the guerrillas attending the FARC's Constitutive Conference in 1966 to

> examine our faults, of which there were naturally more than a few. We were still not achieving the necessary synchronization and coherence in our military work and political activities. There were still remnants of indiscipline, displays of caudillismo and blatant contempt for criticism. We were not adequately challenging the political work of the reactionary sectors. We were showing deficiencies in the political-military capabilities of our cadres and rank-and-file

combatants. Some cases of bad behaviour toward the peasants and friendly political organizations had come up. All this needed to be corrected.[16]

The FARC established its military structures, which would eventually consist of a Secretariat containing seven members including the group's supreme commander. Next in the chain of command is the Central High Command, which consists of approximately thirty guerrillas and below that are the seven blocs of the FARC, each of which operate in different regions of the country. Within each bloc are fronts, columns, platoons and the smallest unit, squads, which consist of twelve fighters. Upon its forming, the undisputed leaders of the FARC were Marulanda and Arenas. As the US Army's Major Jon-Paul Maddaloni would later note in his analysis of the FARC, 'Marulanda's abilities were as a strong guerrilla fighter and charismatic leader, while Arenas was the intellectual Marxist ideologue. Together they formed a formidable team and attracted the disenfranchised agrarian poor and socialist leaning rebels to their cause.'[17]

Historian Marco Palacios suggests that the FARC's 'collective level of organization, discipline, and cultivation of local support networks far exceeded anything the Colombian military had seen in its successful extermination of Liberal and Conservative guerrilla holdouts from the Violencia'.[18] Palacios also argues that the successes of the FARC during its early years proved beneficial to the PCC:

> With the growth of the FARC the Communist Party won some degree of prestige, or at least notoriety at home and abroad, as its 'armed wing' was both stronger and more peasant-dominated than any of its rivals at home or comrade organizations in the region.[19]

Several other guerrilla groups influenced by the Cuban Revolution also emerged in the mid-1960s with the same objective of overthrowing the National Front government. Foremost among them were the aforementioned ELN and the Popular Liberation Army (Ejército Popular de Liberación, EPL). These groups, according to Palacios, 'sought to build on two exclusions. First, the social exclusion of the rural poor, which the agrarian reform of the 1960s did nothing to address; second, the political exclusion represented by the two-party National Front.'[20]

The ELN and EPL were led by urban middle-class intellectuals, whereas the FARC's leadership, with the exception of the urban working-class Arenas, consisted of peasants. As sociologist Eduardo Pizarro has noted, unlike these other guerrilla groups, the FARC did not arise from a 'strictly voluntarist decision or as a mechanical effort to transplant the Cuban Revolution.... the FARC emerged as a people's response to official violence and militarist aggression.'[21] Initially, argue economist Frank Safford and Palacios, the peasants had taken up arms simply to defend themselves from armed groups that served the interests of large landowners, but 'government attacks transformed the peasant self-defense organizations into revolutionary guerrillas'.[22] Meanwhile, Robert Drexler noted that 'guerrilla forces operated in isolated parts of rural Colombia where they sought to exploit appalling local poverty and the inability or unwillingness of the National Front governments to address the basic needs of a long-suffering population.'[23]

The Agrarian Crisis

In 1961, the Colombian Congress had passed the Agrarian Social Reform Law (Law 135), which was supposed to 'address the basic needs of a long-suffering population' by helping peasants obtain legal title to their land and gain access to credit. It was also intended to be a mechanism for addressing the grossly unequal distribution of arable land through expropriation and redistribution. In 1960, a mere 1.7 per cent of landowners owned 55 per cent of Colombia's arable land, while 62.5 per cent of the country's farmers subsisted on less than 1 per cent of the national territory suitable for agriculture.[24] The stated objective of Law 135 was to address this gross inequality in land distribution. In essence, Law 135 was intended as the 'carrot' that complemented the Plan LASO counter-insurgency 'stick'.

Ten years after its enactment, however, Law 135 had resulted in less than 1 per cent of the land that qualified for expropriation being redistributed, and the majority of that was state-owned land.[25] For the most part, the latifundios, or large estates, owned by the country's major landowners were exempted from the agrarian reform law. Furthermore, the legal hoops that peasants were forced to jump through in order to obtain title and credit often prevented them from achieving the desired security over their property. In fact, during the decade that Law 135 was in effect, land ownership became even more concentrated in the hands of large landowners. Many peasants that were forced from their lands contributed to the urbanization process that Colombia was undergoing as they relocated to the cities in search of employment. However, an economic recession in the mid-1960s saw urban unemployment levels jump from 4.9 per cent in 1964 to 13 per cent three years later.[26]

Many peasants responded to the triple threat of state repression, failed agrarian reform policies and growing urban unemployment by instigating their own agrarian reform through the colonization of the Amazon region in eastern and southern Colombia. In 1964, some 375,000 peasants migrated to the colonized zones, where they laid claim to land and proceeded to cut down the rainforest in order to farm. Among these *colonos* were the armed peasants that founded the FARC. Many of the *colonos* soon became affiliated with the guerrillas in order to defend themselves against aggression by the state and large landowners. In fact, the FARC became the most effective form of defence for many peasants. According to author Alfredo Molano, 'In the zones where the FARC had no influence in the 1960s, the process of dismantling peasant colonization and transferring land to large landowning interests proceeded without interference.'[27]

Armed peasants belonging to the FARC did more than simply defend their land since, as previously mentioned, they also formulated their own agrarian reform programme, in July 1964. According to the FARC,

> we put forward an effective revolutionary agrarian policy that would change the social structure of the Colombian countryside, providing land completely free to the peasants who work it or want to work it on the basis of confiscation of large landholdings for the benefit of all working people.[28]

The FARC's Agrarian Reform Programme of the Guerrillas states:

> The Revolutionary Agrarian Policy is the indispensible condition to raise the standard of material and cultural life of the whole peasantry, free it from unemployment, hunger, illiteracy and the endemic illnesses that limit its ability to work, to eliminate the fetters of the large landholding system.[29]

It declares that peasants will receive title to the land they work and that the size of landholding will be determined in accordance with the fertility and location of the property.[30]

The Programme also states that 'Indigenous communities shall be protected, providing them sufficient land for their development... At the same time, an autonomous organization of these communities shall be established, respecting their councils, way of life, culture, languages and internal organization.'[31] In the ensuing decades, the FARC's relationship with Colombia's indigenous peoples would vary dramatically from region to region. In some areas, the guerrillas and indigenous would coexist in relative harmony. In other regions, particularly where the indigenous demanded that FARC fighters not enter their traditional lands, the guerrillas often failed to respect the rights of the communities.

The FARC's Early Strategy

Given the FARC's peasant roots, it is not surprising that its first important programme related to agrarian reform. However, the vision of the guerrillas extended beyond the countryside and was influenced by more than their existential reality at the repressive hands of the state.

The FARC's approach is intrinsically linked to its roots in the peasant self-defence organizations during La Violencia. Those roots pre-date the Cuban Revolution and, in contrast to most of the guerrilla groups that formed throughout Latin America during the 1960s and 1970s, the FARC did not initially adhere to Che Guevara's foco theory. According to Guevara's theory, small guerrilla units act as a vanguard and through armed struggle help create the conditions necessary for revolution. The masses would then follow their example and institute a popular uprising to overthrow the national government. This was the theory utilized by guerrilla movements throughout the region, including the Farabundo Martí National Liberation Front (Frente Farabundo Martí para la Liberación Nacional, FMLN) in El Salvador, the Sandinista National Liberation Front (Frente Sandinista de Liberación Nacional, FSLN) in Nicaragua, as well as by Colombia's ELN. Each of these guerrilla groups was formed following the Cuban Revolution by leaders who were urban middle-class intellectuals. While each eventually obtained significant support and membership from the peasantry, their leadership positions remained in the hands of a university-educated vanguard from the cities.

In contrast, the FARC was founded by peasants and most of its leaders have come from the peasantry. As such, the FARC is unique among contemporary guerrilla organizations in Latin America. Rather than its founders acting as a revolutionary vanguard that sought to motivate the peasantry into engaging in armed revolutionary struggle, the FARC was formed by an already politicized peasantry responding to existing conditions and seeking to defend itself against state repression.

By the 1970s, the FARC was extending its military presence to rural regions throughout the country, particularly in Caldas, Cundinamarca, Antioquia, Cauca and the middle Magdalena, as well as expanding its existing presence in Tolima and Huila. The deployment of FARC fronts across rural Colombia, according to Molano, 'accentuated the political component of the program and allowed the ideological orientation of the Communist party to be emphasized.... The social and economic organization of these regions developed somewhat independent of the military organization, which was always organized and efficient.'[32] Between 1970 and 1982, during this period of geographic expansion, the FARC grew from an estimated 500 fighters to a force of 3,000.[33]

In the late 1970s, President Julio César Turbay responded to the growing guerrilla threat by, in the words of US diplomat Robert Drexler, who was based in Bogotá at the time, 'implementing the most repressive regime Colombia had known since Rojas Pinilla'.[34] According to Drexler,

President Turbay invoked a state of siege, signing a national security statute which broadened the armed forces' powers of arrest and placed a wide range of crimes under the jurisdiction of military tribunals.... Soon, the Turbay administration faced widespread charges that the army was engaging in arbitrary arrests, using torture, and causing people to 'disappear' in the worst tradition of Latin American military brutality. Some of these excesses were covered up by the government's severe censorship of the press, but international human rights agencies raised alarms which are still being heard.[35]

Ultimately, Turbay's repressive policies failed to diminish the growing strength of the FARC, particularly in the countryside. The US Army's Major Maddaloni notes that not only did the Turbay administration's policies fail, but

> the Security Statute had an interesting effect on the FARC's recruitment. Throughout this period they earned their reputation as a sort of David against the strong-arm tactics of the government Goliath. This perception increased their romantic rebel image and brought many younger volunteers to their ranks.[36]

Marco Palacios also acknowledged that the FARC was proving successful in many rural regions, but he claimed that the failure of the guerrilla group to engage in conventional political activities on the national level ultimately left it marginalized and politically ineffective. According to Palacios,

> From the beginning the guerrillas chose to isolate themselves from the cultural and political trends of the cities... Guerrilla commanders have not tried to forge stable and systematic alliances with union members, university students, or cultural workers. They have therefore always been weak and marginal in what we might call national politics; but in parts of the countryside they have successfully woven networks of support and sympathy, as have their paramilitary enemies.[37]

Others have argued that such a state-centrist analysis fails to recognize the unique revolutionary approach of the FARC. The FARC's ideological roots are firmly in Marxism–Leninism, while also being influenced by the shifting realities of peasant life in rural Colombia. According to sociologist James J. Brittain, analysts who examine the revolutionary struggle in Colombia through a state-centrist lens often misinterpret the reality in the countryside. The FARC has largely failed to seriously threaten or influence the centralized state based in the capital Bogotá because it has sought to change society from below. In other words, the guerrillas have largely ignored more conventional avenues to transform society, such as elections and engagement with existing national institutions, and instead have worked at the community level and outside the parameters of the nation's traditional power structures.[38]

As sociologist James Petras notes, the 'FARC has built its power base patiently over time with a precise strategic plan: the accumulation of local power.'[39] In short, the FARC was implementing its revolutionary project on the local level without achieving regime change at the national level, although the latter remained a long-term objective of the guerrilla group's revolution from below.

CHAPTER 2

The FARC's Political Front

By the early 1980s, the FARC had become thoroughly entrenched in its traditional strongholds in southern and eastern Colombia and in the south-central highlands. It was operating as a de facto government for rural communities across vast stretches of countryside where the state had never established a presence – other than the occasional military incursion. The guerrilla group was also expanding to other regions as both its number of fighters and its military capacity increased. This period also saw a shift in the FARC's military strategy as well as the emergence of the guerrilla group on the national political scene.

The FARC's Seventh Conference, held in May 1982, was significant in that it led to a change in the group's name and a shift in its military character. The guerrilla group renamed itself the Revolutionary Armed Forces of Colombia – People's Army (Fuerzas Armadas Revolucionarias de Colombia – Ejército del Pueblo, FARC–EP). The shift in the FARC's military strategy called for the group to become more offensive-minded by actively seeking out large-scale confrontations with the state and to expand its areas of operation to medium-sized cities. According to the guerrilla group, 'This was a new way of operating which made the FARC–EP an authentically offensive guerrilla movement. This new method meant that the FARC–EP would no longer wait in ambush for the enemy.'[1]

At the Seventh Conference, the FARC's political leader Jacobo Arenas reaffirmed the group's commitment to a 'combination of all forms of struggle' by calling for an expansion of its political activities. At this time, the FARC's growing military capacity opened the door to the group's involvement in the country's political process at the national level. In November 1982, President Belisario Betancur, a moderate in the Conservative Party, issued an amnesty for all imprisoned guerrillas in the hope of initiating peace talks with the country's various rebel groups. In May 1984, the government and the FARC signed the Uribe Accords, which set the terms for a ceasefire and peace talks. The peace process would later also include the smaller EPL rebel group and the more moderate M-19, which had formed in the early 1970s. The ELN, on the other hand, refused to participate in the talks. As sociologist Ricardo Vargas points out, by addressing some of the FARC's socio-economic demands, 'Betancur's position was a radical departure from that of his predecessors, for he recognized that guerrilla violence was the product of real social conditions and he understood the relationship between those conditions and the demands of the insurgents.'[2]

While the Uribe Accords instituted a ceasefire, it allowed the guerrillas to retain their military structures and weapons. The FARC adhered to the ceasefire, but the M-19 dropped out of the process and resumed military operations the following year with its disastrous takeover of the country's Supreme Court, known as the Palace of Justice, located in central Bogotá. The army responded to the takeover by shelling and levelling the massive courthouse, causing the deaths of more than a hundred people, including eleven Supreme Court justices. The M-19 would never fully recover from the Palace of Justice debacle.

The Patriotic Union

As for the FARC, it used the peace process as a means to expand its political influence when, with the help of the Communist Party, it established the Patriotic Union (Unión Patriótica, UP) party. The UP attracted many on the left who sought an alternative to the two dominant parties that, despite the formal end of the National Front in 1974, continued to maintain a stranglehold on the country's political scene. Arenas and a young FARC commander named Alfonso Cano were responsible for meeting with the government's emissaries in the lead-up to the signing of the Uribe Accords and the creation of the UP. While Arenas had been the FARC's political leader since the guerrilla group's inception, Cano was a relatively new recruit. He was an urban intellectual with a history of organizing with the Communist Party. Arenas and Cano told the government's emissaries that the FARC was willing to engage in both peace talks and the political process, but that the rebel group was not willing to demobilize because it did not trust that the government would not respond as it had during La Violencia, when it began killing amnestied Liberal guerrillas.

The UP was launched in 1985 and the FARC saw the party as a mechanism through which the guerrilla group could increase its presence in urban areas and get its political message out to the general population. The FARC's Seventh Conference had concluded with a call for the establishment of 'solidarity cells' as a means for organizing the population in rural and urban areas. As author Steven Dudley notes, 'Originally, these were to be clandestine cells. But with the UP, they could work in the open.

The advantages were immeasurable. They could sell the FARC's ideas, organize political rallies for rebel leaders, and recruit new members in public.'³

Arenas ordered FARC fronts to organize and educate peasants in rural municipalities, while urban intellectuals, students and unionists rallied support in the cities. Each FARC front had a *político*, or political representative, who was responsible for educating both the guerrillas and the rural population. In addition to teaching basic literacy skills, the *político* would also provide a political education. Additionally, FARC units would go from village to village and hold assemblies to inform the people about the UP and to encourage them to create a *Junta Patriótica*, or patriotic cell, which would then represent the party on the community level. According to Dudley,

> War and politics were coming together to make way for hope. The FARC inspired this confidence, and it presented itself as a ready replacement for an absentee government.... and the UP began to creep into the national political scene. By election time two years later, the FARC had organized four thousand *Juntas Patrióticas*.⁴

In March 1986, local and congressional elections were held in which the UP ended up with 24 provincial deputies and 275 municipal representatives on the local level, in addition to having 4 senators and 4 congressional representatives – including two FARC members, Iván Márquez and Braulio Herrera – elected nationally. And while the Liberal Party's Virgilio Barco won the presidential election handily two months later, the UP's candidate Jaime Pardo Leal, a lawyer and long-time member of the Communist Party, garnered 328,752 votes, the most ever received by a leftist candidate up until that time.⁵ The UP's performance in both local and national elections far surpassed all expectations, given the newness of the party and its relative lack of resources.

For the first time in Colombia's history, a leftist party had established a notable presence on the country's political scene. In the eyes of Colombia's traditional ruling class, the events of the previous few years had transformed the FARC from a minor annoyance situated in remote rural regions to a serious threat to the nation.

The Reactionary Response

In 1965, the Colombian government had issued a decree in order to implement the aforementioned proposals of the US Army calling for the establishment of paramilitaries to combat the emerging guerrilla threat. Three years later, the passage of Law 48 enshrined the military's legal right to organize and arm civilian 'self-defence' units.[6] The military's use of Law 48 was sporadic throughout the 1970s, but it responded to Betancur's peace initiatives in the mid-1980s by intensifying its creation of paramilitary groups. Because the ceasefire under the Uribe Accords prohibited the military from engaging in counter-insurgency operations, the army began relying on its new paramilitary allies not only to target guerrillas, but also to wage a 'dirty war' against the non-violent left, particularly members of the newly formed UP. The new paramilitary groups were also supported and funded by drug traffickers, large landowners and the business sector.

The Colombian army established a paramilitary organization in Puerto Boyacá, in the northern department of Santander, under the auspices of the town's military mayor, Captain Oscar de Jesús Echandía. According to Human Rights Watch,

> In 1982, Echandía convened a meeting of local people, including local Liberal and Conservative party leaders, businessmen, ranchers, and representatives from the Texas Petroleum Company. They found that their goal went far beyond protecting the population from

guerrilla demands. They wanted to 'cleanse' [*limpiar*] the region of subversives.[7]

Civilians were hired and armed in order to perform the 'cleansing', with logistical support provided by the military. The following year, the army formed the 14th Brigade in the same region. According to Dudley, 'the brigade would become the epicenter of paramilitary activity providing information and cover for the paramilitary groups that had amassed in the region.'[8]

It quickly became apparent that newly elected President Barco had little interest in continuing the peace process initiated by his predecessor Betancur. As a result, the peace talks collapsed in 1987 and the war between the FARC and the government resumed. The military and its paramilitary allies responded to the UP's electoral successes by decimating the party. In October 1987, Pardo Leal, the UP's presidential candidate in the previous year's election, was assassinated. The paramilitaries not only targeted the UP's leaders; they also sought to eliminate its grassroots activists and organizers. Each year, several hundred UP members would be killed, and in 1988, when the party's candidates proved victorious in sixteen mayoral elections, three of the victors were immediately assassinated.

In the midst of the bloodbath, some sectors within the UP began suggesting that the party sever its affiliation with the FARC in an attempt to protect members from the slaughter. Hardliners in the party argued that a separation from the FARC would do little to diminish the threat against the UP because the paramilitaries would target any leftist, whether violent or non-violent, that they saw as posing a threat to the political and economic interests of the country's ruling elite.

Ideology was also a factor in the debate since the party had attracted increasing numbers of centre-leftists who did not support the armed struggle and who were more social-democratic than

socialist. Bernardo Jaramillo, who replaced Pardo Leal as the
UP's leader, became increasingly aligned with the more moderate
faction during his first two years as the party's president. This
inevitably placed him at odds with both the Communist Party
and the FARC. Jaramillo and moderates in the party believed
that Soviet premier Mikhail Gorbachev's reforms, known as *peres-
troika*, and the collapse of the Berlin Wall meant that socialism
was no longer a viable objective.

The FARC and the Communist Party, on the other hand,
saw things very differently. The guerrilla group reiterated its
Marxist–Leninist principles and noted:

> The validity of the armed struggle is not determined by whether the
> Berlin wall fell or not; it is determined by the reality of our country
> and here, the political, economic and social disequilibrium and the
> state violence that impelled the rebellion, continue in place.[9]

Consequently, the UP found itself in a dilemma. According to
Dudley,

> If the party denounced the FARC for refusing to lay down its weap-
> ons, then it would lose credibility with many of its followers and
> its rebel sponsors. If it didn't denounce the guerrilla group, the
> opposition would vilify it. All the pieces were falling into place for
> a 'political genocide'.[10]

While the party's internal debate about its future continued, so
did the killings. And when Jaramillo was asked how he thought
he would die, the UP leader simply stated, 'They're going to kill
me on any corner, at any moment. It could even be in my house. I
know they're going to kill me.'[11] And, sure enough, Jaramillo was
gunned down in Bogotá airport in March 1990 while campaigning
for the upcoming presidential election.

Five years after the UP's founding, it was clear that a
'political genocide' was indeed taking place. In addition to its

two presidential candidates, four elected congressmen and more than two thousand members of the UP were assassinated during that five-year period. The exodus of party members from the UP that had been occurring due to the relentless assassinations turned into a stampede after Jaramillo was killed. Some party members simply dropped out of politics, others went underground or into exile, and many fled into the jungle to join the FARC, convinced that the decimation of the UP was proof that armed struggle was the only option remaining to achieve social justice in Colombia.

Meanwhile, one month after Jaramillo was killed, Carlos Pizarro, the presidential candidate of the new Democratic Alliance M-19 political party, was also assassinated. Having failed to recover militarily from the failed takeover of the Palace of Justice, the M-19 guerrilla group had decided to lay down its arms and demobilize under a peace agreement that called for the group to transition itself to a political party. Pizarro's death appeared to vindicate the fears expressed by hardliners in the FARC and the Communist Party that separating the UP from the guerrilla group would not eliminate the threat faced by the party's members. After all, the M-19, which was far more moderate than both the FARC and the UP, had laid down its weapons to engage in the political process and still its leaders were being assassinated.

Twenty years after Jaramillo's assassination, the inspector general of Colombia would declare that Alberto Romero, the head of the country's intelligence agency, the Department of Administrative Security (Departamento Administrativo de Seguridad, DAS), and paramilitary leader Carlos Castaño were the co-authors of the crime.[12] Meanwhile, five months after Jaramillo's death, the UP's ideological founder, Arenas, died of cancer, fully aware that his political project was in its own death throes.

A Return to War

In 1987, following the breakdown of the peace talks with the Betancur administration and the end of the ceasefire, the FARC had not only returned to waging war against the state; it had also joined the Simón Bolívar Guerrilla Coordinating Committee (Coordinadora Guerrillera Simón Bolívar, CGSB) along with Colombia's other armed insurgent groups.[13] The idea was to present a united political and military front. But by the end of the decade, the M-19, the EPL and several smaller and militarily weak guerrilla groups were negotiating their demobilizations with the government in order to form political parties to engage in elections for a Constituent Assembly. As of 1990, the FARC, ELN and a small dissident faction of the EPL were the only remaining members of the CGSB.

In December 1990, the M-19's newly formed political party, the Democratic Alliance M-19, won the most delegates in the Constituent Assembly. A new and progressive constitution was voted into existence in 1991, which provided important rights to minority groups such as the indigenous and Afro-Colombians. But while the new constitution called for a much more participatory democracy on paper, the country's two traditional parties continued to dominate the political scene and ensured that the reality on the ground changed little for the majority of Colombians.

The role played by demobilized guerrillas in drawing up the new constitution led many Colombians, even on the left, to question the validity of armed struggle – particularly in a post-Cold War context in which guerrilla groups throughout Latin America were laying down their arms in order to participate in electoral processes. Many people began viewing the FARC as a Cold War relic, an archaic Marxist–Leninist organization.

In this context, negotiators for the CGSB met with representatives of the government of Liberal President César Gaviria
in Caracas, Venezuela, and in Tlaxcala, Mexico, in 1991 and 1992
respectively. The talks were exploratory in nature, examining
the possibility of launching a formal peace process. The CGSB
insisted on a twelve-point negotiating agenda in order for formal
peace talks to be initiated. The twelve points called for addressing the implementation of neoliberal, or so-called free-market,
economic policies in Colombia; human rights; the exploitation of
the country's natural resources; and a restructuring of the armed
forces and the political system. As Alfredo Molano noted,

> In Mexico, the CGSB succeeded in placing a debate about the neo-
> liberal model on the agenda, and the government's economic team
> came to the negotiations to justify the Washington Consensus of
> free trade and privatization. The guerrilla team questioned every
> aspect of the Consensus, even as business associations and the right
> complained that it was unnecessary and offensive for the government
> to have to justify its economic policies before a group of 'gangsters.'
> For their part, government spokespeople argued that significant
> economic changes were impossible, since Colombia was now part of
> a globalized economy that imposed its own obligatory rules.[14]

Ultimately, the exploratory talks broke down and President
Gaviria declared that the implementation of the new constitution
eliminated any justification for armed struggle. So far as the
government was concerned there was little to negotiate beyond
the logistics involved in the demobilization of the guerrillas,
as had occurred with the M-19 and with other rebel groups in
Central America such as the FMLN in El Salvador. But in the
eyes of the FARC, it was essential that a negotiated settlement to
the conflict go 'beyond the narrow approach of the government
which attempted to reduce peace to the mere cessation of armed
struggle'.[15]

An important contributing factor to the failure of the exploratory talks, as Molano noted, was the government's refusal to negotiate the neoliberal economic model being implemented in Colombia. Additionally, US diplomat Drexler noted that

> opposition to reconciliation and to the reintegration of the guerrillas remains strong among ultraconservatives and the armed forces. The progress achieved by President Gaviria was accompanied by continual attempts to sabotage his policies including, as we have noted, the assassination of guerrilla leaders and other leftists after they have signed accords and attempted to participate in the normal political life of the nation.[16]

Almost a decade later, in 1999, the twelve points of negotiation would again constitute the foundation of the FARC's proposals in peace talks with the government of President Andrés Pastrana. And, once again, the intransigence of the government with regard to negotiating the country's neoliberal policies, along with the military's opposition to a political solution to the conflict, would play major roles in the collapse of that peace process.

The breakdown in the talks between the CGSB and the government also led to the termination of the guerrilla groups' political coalition. The three guerrilla groups once again began acting independently, and in April 1993 the FARC held its Eighth Conference at its stronghold in La Uribe in the department of Meta. The FARC issued a political declaration at the Eighth Conference that included a scathing attack on the neoliberal policies that had recently been initiated in Colombia:

> Executing the directives of the IMF [International Monetary Fund], the government of the dictator Gaviria precipitously opens our borders and internal market to big foreign capital and production. It privatizes important state enterprises and entities, lays off workers and other employees en masse, guarantees broad benefits to the owner-speculators of finance capital, removes incentives for

agricultural production and puts national producers into bankrupt-
cy.... This is the development of savage capitalism, of neo-liberalism
in which economic growth opposes social well-being.[17]

The FARC and the PCC officially split at the Eighth Conference, although in actuality the two organizations had been
functioning independently from each other since the late 1980s.
During the 1990s, there was also a growing split between the
FARC and many among the country's urban intellectual left.
Peasants had always constituted the primary support base for the
FARC, but its ties to the PCC and UP had helped the guerrilla
group establish backing from sectors of the urban intellectual
left. However, the slaughter of the UP, the split with the mostly
urban-based PCC, and the growing numbers of urban leftist
intellectuals questioning the validity of armed struggle in the
post-Soviet era made it evident that the FARC had once again
become a primarily rural-based organization.

Two additional factors that contributed to the FARC's growing
isolation from the urban left was the intensification of the dirty
war being waged in the cities by paramilitaries and the fact that
the guerrilla group's political agenda remained focused mostly on
rural issues that did not resonate with the urban middle class.
As sociologist Nazih Richani noted,

> The dialogue between the guerrillas and the majority of leftist intel-
> lectuals was practically severed in the 1990s. Consequently, the
> guerrillas lost an important political conduit in urban centers, which
> weakened their abilities to mobilize within the cities.[18]

In 2000, the guerrilla group sought to revitalize its influence in the country's cities by launching a new political party
called the Clandestine Colombian Communist Party (PCCC)
as part of its Bolivarian Movement for a New Colombia. FARC
commander Cano, who had replaced Arenas in the guerrilla

group's Secretariat and as its political leader, was responsible for the new party. Cano sought to establish PCCC cells in urban areas throughout the country. Shortly after the launching of the PCCC and the Bolivarian Movement for a New Colombia, FARC Commander Simón Trinidad explained that, in light of what happened to the UP, the guerrilla group had no choice but to engage in political activities clandestinely. The new party is, according to Trinidad,

> A political movement that works to recover Colombian society in secret, a movement that's militant and clandestine. There will be campesinos, students, workers, women and intellectuals who will fight the political confrontation without saying they belong to the Bolivarian Movement. They will not participate in elections because there are no guarantees and conditions that they will not be killed.[19]

Because of its clandestine nature, it is difficult to determine how successful the FARC has been with this venture. It is much more challenging for the PCCC and FARC militias to operate in urban areas than in the countryside due to the prominent presence of state security forces. As a result, many social activists and representatives of civil society organizations working in the poor barrios of Bogotá have been accused of being members of the PCCC, and some have been imprisoned or killed.

The FARC's role in national political affairs peaked with the successes of the UP during the mid-1980s, and faded quickly with the decimation of that party. While struggling throughout the 1990s to recapture the national exposure on the political front that it had enjoyed with the UP, the FARC also returned to the battlefield where it achieved its greatest military successes and sought to consolidate its control over rural regions of the country.

CHAPTER 3

The FARC's Social Project

WHILE THE FARC was struggling to regain its political influence amongst leftist circles in Colombia's urban centres during the 1990s, its control over rural regions was expanding significantly. Much of this expansion was military in nature, but the rebel group also implemented social projects in many regions, particularly in its traditional strongholds. Colombia's dire economic condition not only ensured the FARC a steady stream of recruits, it also led to increasing numbers of Colombians migrating to rebel-controlled regions, particularly in the east and south of the country, where they lived under FARC rule.

During the National Front years, the percentage of the nation's workforce living in absolute poverty had more than doubled, from 25 to 51 per cent. The figures were even worse for rural labourers, where the rate of absolute poverty soared from 25 to 68 per cent.[1] With so many Colombians living under such dire conditions, it is no surprise that the cocaine boom in the late 1970s initiated a migration of urban unemployed and landless peasants to predominantly FARC-controlled regions to cultivate the coca plant, which provides the raw ingredient for cocaine.

The FARC functioned as a de facto government in the regions under its control, particularly in its traditional strongholds in eastern and southern Colombia. In that role, the guerrillas provided social services and maintained law and order over the growing population through the implementation of their own judicial system. According to Richani,

> For these services the FARC imposes a progressive income taxation system. Poor peasants are mostly exempted from this tax. FARC levies, for example, a beer tax and the revenues are used to support local schools and other projects. Usually an elected committee from the locality decides on disbursement and allocation of the taxes collected.[2]

While the FARC imposes local taxes at the community level, it also applies national taxes to wealthy individuals and businesses regardless of where they are located in Colombia. As a communiqué from the rebel group's Secretariat made clear in May 1995:

> On the subject of finances, we continue with our policy of collecting the 'tax for New Colombia' from those natural or legal enemies of democracy whose wealth is in excess of one billion pesos. Our struggle is against an unjust state and against the rich who support and make use of it. If these persons give money to the state to carry on the war against the people, they also must give it to the people for its defence against the aggression.[3]

Six years later, FARC commander Raúl Reyes explained that under the rebel group's Law 002, any individual or business in Colombia with assets worth $1 million or more was required to pay a tax:

> We have been charging this tax. And the people pay it because they know they have to do so. There are others who do not want to pay the tax and they are the 'tax evaders'. Because the FARC has no jails, these people are held until they pay. They are the ones we are said to have kidnapped.[4]

From the perspective of the FARC, what is commonly referred to as 'extortion' is simply a war tax imposed on the wealthy by the guerrillas; 'kidnap victims' are merely those who have been retained for non-payment of taxes; and the 'ransom' paid for their release simply constitutes the payment of tax arrears.

The FARC's system of taxation is basically two-tiered. The income from taxing drug production and trafficking in the regions under its control, as well as the income earned from extorting and kidnapping wealthy individuals and businesses under Law 002, is used to fund the FARC's military operations. Meanwhile, the revenues generated from taxes imposed on local businesses in FARC-controlled regions is turned over to community leaders and used to fund social, economic and infrastructure projects.[5]

During the 1990s, many small towns in remote regions of eastern and southern Colombia experienced significant infrastructure improvements as a result of the FARC's public works programmes. The FARC built hundreds of miles of roads that connected dozens of communities to each other. In 2003, Efrain Salazar, the FARC's public works director in Meta, claimed to have an annual budget of $1 million and to pay those civilians who worked for him a monthly salary of $125.[6]

The Colombian military's targeting of bridges built by the FARC have highlighted the challenges posed by engaging in social and infrastructure projects as a non-state actor in the middle of an armed conflict. In 2003, the Colombian air force bombed the largest bridge ever built by the guerrillas, a 70 foot long and 40 foot high structure that spanned the Yarumales Canyon in Meta, which cost $110,000 to construct.[7] While such attacks against infrastructure hinder the FARC's ability to move around the region, they also prove devastating to peasants who are dependent on it for getting crops to markets.

The Role of JACs

Some sympathizers of the FARC have suggested that the guerrillas not engage in social projects and instead focus all of their energy and resources on the armed struggle. One community leader in the department of Valle de Cauca argued:

> [I]t is my personal belief that the FARC should not provide social services at this stage in the struggle. It is not their responsibility to offer, provide, or distribute social services for they are not the state.... The most important service that the FARC provides is their support for the struggle of the people through the defense of our rights and needs for change. It is through our Acción Comunal that the services are to be provided and through the FARC–EP that our communities can exist to do so.[8]

The Acción Comunal that the community leader referred to is one of thousands of locally elected Communal Action Committees (Juntas de Acción Comunal, JACs) that exist throughout Colombia. The JACs were initially established by the government in the early years of the National Front in order to undermine the appeal of more radical political forces among the peasantry, such as the Colombian Communist Party and the Cuban Revolution. The objective was to form community action boards comprising local residents that would be responsible for local development projects, such as the building of schools and health clinics, the installation of water supply systems and sewers, and low-cost housing and other infrastructure. The JACs were not, however, permitted to wield any political power, which remained firmly in the hands of municipal governments loyal to the Liberal and Conservative parties.

During the ensuing decades, many JACs became increasingly politicized, particularly in remote rural regions that remained largely neglected by the national government and where poverty persisted. In southern and eastern Colombia in particular, many JACs established close relationships with the FARC and, ultimately, became the body responsible for managing the local taxes collected by the guerrillas. Government decisions to cut off funding to JACs deemed to be too radical only served to push them even closer to the guerrillas.

So while some FARC fronts have been directly involved in organizing social and infrastructure projects, others simply ensure that local JACs are sufficiently funded so they can, as the community leader in Valle de Cauca suggested, provide public services. In the late 1990s, for example, the FARC ensured that the local JAC in the town of La Cooperativa in Meta received enough of the guerrilla group's tax revenues to construct an electricity grid, to which the homes of each of the town's 400 residents became connected. The local JAC funded the maintenance of the grid – including the purchase of fuel for the large generator – by organizing fiestas several times a year and utilizing the money generated from ticket and alcohol sales. It was relatively easy for the JAC to raise the necessary revenues to maintain the system because the town was a bustling commercial and social centre due to the region's booming coca economy. Local residents mingled freely with uniformed, rifle-toting guerrillas in the streets, stores and restaurants.[9]

But in 2007, a Colombian military offensive pushed the guerrillas out of the region and decimated the local coca economy. The arrival of the army and the resulting economic downturn displaced 80 per cent of the residents of La Cooperativa and surrounding villages. The local JAC could no longer maintain the electricity grid due to a lack of funding and the government refused to cover the cost of running the generator. The remaining local residents had to re-adapt to life without electricity.[10]

A similar process in which the FARC generates revenues for local JACs has also occurred in cities, including Barrancabermeja, where

US-based Westinghouse and an Italian company called Technipetrol were contracted by the government to construct a power plant in 1997. The FARC demanded that the companies provide $2 million in funding to construct a vocational school to train youths from poor neighbourhoods and another $150,000 for a project to generate 200 jobs. In this instance, the FARC did not directly collect the 'tax' money, but rather facilitated its delivery to the local JAC, which then oversaw the projects. In return for the funding, the companies and their employees were allowed to operate in Barrancabermeja without further harassment from the guerrillas.[11] Similarly in Remolinos del Caguán in Caquetá, the FARC ensured that the local JAC received the revenues from a tax the guerrilla group imposed on beer sales in order to build a new school.[12]

The guerrillas have also implemented their version of revolutionary justice in their traditional strongholds. For example, during the years (1999–2002) when the FARC was given a safe haven in which to negotiate with the Pastrana government, peasants would line up outside a makeshift rebel courtroom on the outskirts of San Vicente del Caguán in the department of Caquetá. One by one they would file into the courtroom and make a formal complaint to the FARC judge. The judge would then issue a summons to the other party ordering them to come to the courthouse and present their version of the story. If the two sides were unable to reach a settlement then the judge would issue a ruling. Any failure to abide by a judge's ruling would result in expulsion from the rebel-controlled region.

Most complaints are related to land and business disputes, although family issues, such as non-payment of child support, are also commonly addressed. There have been cases of wives bringing complaints against their husbands for spending most of the family's income on alcohol and not leaving enough money to purchase milk and food for the children. In such instances, the FARC's justice system has become an efficient mechanism through which women can defend their rights.

Many peasants prefer guerrilla justice to the endemic corruption and inefficiency that have plagued the country's government-run legal system. One woman waiting to see a FARC judge in Caquetá explained why she preferred the guerrilla group's model of justice over the government's system: 'It's better than before because it's easier, faster and less corrupt. Two parties can present their cases and there is always a solution. If one party doesn't have the money to pay the fine, then they can make payments over time.'[13] Meanwhile, a peasant in Meta who worked for a local JAC explained how the FARC resolved disputes between people in that region.

> When two people have a disagreement, the rebels listen to both sides and impose a settlement if the two parties cannot reach a satisfactory resolution on their own. Those convicted of serious offences such as fighting or disorderly conduct are forced to work on cooperative farms or fixing the roads.[14]

For the most serious crimes, such as murder and rape, the FARC would sometimes apply the death penalty.

The FARC has also overseen agrarian reform projects in its traditional strongholds, including promoting agricultural co-operatives. During 2002 and 2003, the FARC broke up ten large ranches in the southern part of Meta. The smaller properties were then distributed to subsistence farmers.[15] The guerrillas have carried out similar agrarian reform projects in Caquetá, Putumayo and other regions. The objective of these initiatives is not simply to redistribute land from the wealthy to the poor, but also to lay the foundation for transforming the agricultural model, including preparing peasants for a shift away from coca dependence.

Many farmers are compelled to cultivate coca due to decades of government neglect. The failure of the state to provide the necessary infrastructure to allow farmers to transport perishable food crops to distant markets has made coca the only viable cash crop in many remote regions. Even if farmers manage to get their food crops to market, there is no guarantee that they will earn a living from their sale. On the other hand, coca can be harvested several times each year and cocaine processors eagerly purchase all that is produced, thereby providing peasants with a reliable cash income so they can buy those necessities they cannot grow.

While the FARC permits peasants to supplement their food crops with the income earned from cultivating coca, it has simultaneously sought to implement alternative rural economic models. This has proven particularly challenging because many farmers were formerly impoverished city dwellers who colonized remote rural areas in order to cultivate coca, or newer generation farmers whose parents long ago quit cultivating traditional crops. Consequently, many farmers have little or no knowledge about how to grow traditional crops. According to FARC commander Simón Trinidad:

> We are planning a different solution for the problem of narco-trafficking. It consists of providing a better life for the poor campesino through agrarian reform, by giving them good lands, technical assistance and low-interest loans to change from growing illicit crops to legal crops, such as coffee, yucca, bananas, sugarcane and ranching. An alternative development that facilitates commercialization for these products. But it's a slow process to change them, it's not just destroying the illicit crops and then telling them to grow different ones. We have to educate the campesinos about how to produce them. Give them tools, credits and time so they can make a living from these crops and become a different kind of campesino.[16]

In some parts of Caquetá, the FARC has required coca growers to devote three acres to traditional food crops for every seven acres of coca that they cultivate. In other regions, the guerrillas have introduced a crop ratio programme that limits coca to no more than 25 per cent of a farmer's total cultivation.[17] In short, the FARC is attempting to oversee a return to traditional farming practices for farmers. And because the lack of infrastructure inhibits the ability of many peasants to engage in the formal market – either the domestic or international market – the FARC is helping them to sell their crops by facilitating the trade of surplus goods between JACs within the same region.[18]

A War of Position

According to sociologist James J. Brittain, the FARC's role as a de facto government in many remote regions of eastern and southern Colombia constitutes a counter-hegemonic shift through the guerrilla group's implementation of a Gramscian 'war of position'. Because of the decentralized nature of Colombia's political and economic structures, which themselves have largely been a response to the country's diverse geography consisting of three Andean mountain ranges and vast expanses of rainforest, the FARC has focused primarily on seeking local power in the regions in which it is dominant. The FARC has patiently consolidated its control over vast rural regions where it has taken on many of the responsibilities traditionally performed by a state in areas such as health care, the judiciary and infrastructure building.

Brittain argues that 'a war of position is the most realistic avenue for revolutionary success because of the country's distinctive decentralized political-economic structure.… In light of this, Gramsci's theory can be adapted to fit the Colombian dynamic as the FARC–EP creates pre-revolutionary rural-based centers of dual power at a grassroots level'.[19] In other words, rather than primarily focusing on achieving national power through military means in order to then implement socio-economic changes from above, the FARC is attempting to build a revolution from the grassroots level upward in regions under its control.

But some communities, particularly in northern Colombia, opted to take an alternative approach in the mid-1990s by formulating a new form of resistance and declaring themselves 'peace communities'. In 1997, San José de Apartadó and surrounding hamlets in the Urabá region of northern Colombia were the first community to declare themselves a peace community. As a result, explains Amnesty International,

> Members of the Peace Community refuse to bear arms or to provide information or logistical support to either side. In return they demand that the parties to the conflict do not enter their communities and that they respect their decision not to participate or to collaborate with any of the warring parties.[20]

San José de Apartadó was an important transportation hub and, as a result, guerrilla and paramilitary fighters would often pass through the community. In addition, there was an army base located nearby. During the mid-1990s, right-wing paramilitaries waged a particularly brutal dirty war throughout the region in an effort to eradicate the guerrillas and their sympathizers. The decision by residents of San José de Apartadó to declare themselves a peace community in an effort to escape the violence was not welcomed by any of the armed actors – the FARC, the paramilitaries or the military.

The establishment of the peace community has garnered the residents of San José considerable international exposure and solidarity, but it has failed to protect them from the violence. According to community leaders, 178 community members have been killed since 1997. While the military and paramilitaries have been responsible for the vast majority of the killings, the FARC has been blamed for twenty-four of the deaths as each armed actor has accused members of the community of complicity with their respective enemy.[21]

In 2002, during a visit to the region, President Uribe publicly accused the residents of San José de Apartadó of colluding with guerrillas. Following his accusations, a series of attacks by the military and paramilitaries killed twenty members of the peace community.[22] One of the most infamous attacks against the community occurred in February 2005 when eight villagers, including four children, were massacred and their bodies mutilated. The government immediately blamed the FARC for the massacre, claiming that there were no units from the army's 17th Brigade in the area at the time. However, it was later revealed that a military patrol consisting of a hundred soldiers and fifty paramilitaries was responsible for the killings. In a rare case of justice being carried out in Colombia, one army captain and five paramilitaries were convicted of murder.[23]

While the FARC is actively engaged in community-level social projects in its remote traditional strongholds in eastern and southern Colombia, the peace community in San José de Apartadó illustrates the plight faced by communities situated in regions where all the armed actors maintain a presence. The FARC's social project exists to a much lesser degree – and sometimes not at all – in these regions, where it is not organically linked to the peasantry and where it is mostly preoccupied with its military operations against the Colombian Armed Forces and the paramilitaries. Such was the case in San José de Apartadó before its declaration as a peace community.

Life as a Guerrilla

One option for peasants facing the challenging socio-economic conditions that exist in Colombia's rural regions is to enlist in the FARC itself, which provides them not only with their basic material needs but also with an education. While some peasants join the FARC because of a lack of economic opportunity, others enlist in order to escape repression by the state or paramilitaries. A female guerrilla who goes by the *nom de guerre* Erika joined the FARC at 16 after witnessing a massacre by paramilitaries in her home town in the department of Huila. According to Erika, 'It's a difficult life being a guerrilla. There are lots of sacrifices, like always being away from family.'[24] When asked what her family thought of her decision to join the guerrillas, she replied: 'They agree with it, because they know why we are fighting. But it is hard for my father to accept my being in the FARC because I'm so young.'[25]

There are also peasants who join the guerrillas because they grew up in FARC-controlled regions and admired the rebel fighters. As a guerrilla from Nariño named Jon explains, 'I saw the guerrillas at an early age because they would come to our village and we would give them supplies. They were the only armed group around and I saw being a guerrilla as an attractive way of life.'[26] A female guerrilla who joined the FARC in 1984 at 15 years of age tells a similar story:

> The first time I met the guerrillas was when I was 9 years old, when they came to our house. I almost always lived in zones where the guerrillas were. I had frequent contact with them since they were always coming and going. I decided when I was small that I wanted to be a guerrilla, that it was my destiny.... Since joining, I have been working twenty-four hours a day for the revolution, for the necessary changes for our people, for their welfare, because when you live a civilian life there is no opportunity to study – for education or for health care.[27]

Sometimes when peasants want to join the FARC, the rebel group tells them to join the Colombian military instead so they can act as informants. The FARC attempts to infiltrate units of the army, marines, navy and national police throughout the country in this manner as a means of intelligence-gathering to help the guerrillas defend themselves from upcoming military operations and to plan attacks. Similarly, the Colombian military utilizes the same strategy to infiltrate the FARC's ranks, which means the guerrillas do their best to determine that new recruits are not military informants.

The first thing that every guerrilla does upon joining the FARC is choose a *nom de guerre* in order to protect their family from repercussions. They then receive basic training and political education in one of the FARC's boot camps before being deployed to a full-time unit. Each guerrilla possesses two sets of combat fatigues, a pair of rubber boots, an AK-47 assault rifle and no more personal belongings than are easily transportable.

When the guerrillas are not on the march, they set up camp in remote rainforest or mountain regions. The FARC's jungle camps contain a bivouac for each guerrilla that consists of a bed with wooden planks serving as a mattress, a mosquito net and a plastic camouflaged canopy that hangs above everything to provide protection from the frequent tropical rains. The bivouacs are connected by a network of wooden walkways constructed several inches above the wet, muddy ground. The rebels cut down as few trees as possible during the building of the bivouacs and walkways in order to preserve the rainforest canopy and reduce the possibility of detection from the air. The guerrillas move camp regularly for security reasons, believing that mobility is their best defence against military attack. Such an operation involves packing up everything, except the wooden infrastructure, for the journey to another part of the jungle, where they take out their machetes and begin constructing a new camp. Because the overwhelming majority of the FARC's fighters are peasants, they are very adept with that ubiquitous tool of the countryside, the machete.

The guerrillas get up at 5.00 a.m. every day and all of them – men and women – share equally in performing daily duties such as patrols, guard duty, training exercises and kitchen duty. Guerrilla cooks prepare three meals a day of basic Colombian fare such as beef, chicken, rice, potatoes, yucca, vegetables and soup when supplies are plentiful. However, if the security situation is tense and supplies are difficult to obtain, then they subsist on whatever they can catch in the wild, such as monkeys, snakes and fish. When the guerrillas are not engaged in carrying out one of their many duties, they participate in education programmes that teach basic reading, writing and maths. Many of the guerrillas are poorly educated peasants when they enlist, and some are illiterate. The better-educated rebels are paired with the less literate ones in order to provide them with a basic education and to teach them the fundamental concepts of Marxism. Some of the larger camps have satellite television, in which case, if the security situation allows it, the guerrillas watch the evening news on Colombia's two major television networks, Caracol and RCN. Afterwards they engage in group discussions about current events and political issues. Often they will also watch a movie, usually either a FARC-produced documentary or a Hollywood action flick, before going to bed at 9.00 pm.[28] While life in the FARC is not easy, many guerrillas do have a sense of purpose. As long-time FARC fighter Gladys Marín explains:

> We are not seeking a solution in the style of the Soviet Union, or the style of Cuba, or the style of Vietnam; it's a Colombian thing. We are making our revolution a Colombian one; to make changes, transformations, and to do that we have to overthrow the capitalist government we have today. We need to overthrow it to construct the

society we want. It's a total change of the system, where the people will have housing, education and everything they deserve.[29]

Gender equality is an important component of the FARC's philosophy. In a country where machismo is rampant, particularly in the countryside, guerrilla life often proves empowering to poorly educated peasant women. It is estimated that women constitute 30 per cent of the FARC's fighters, with some attaining high-ranking positions, including commanding entire guerrilla fronts.[30] As one female guerrilla noted, 'Here we have rights and responsibilities to live up to. A woman can find herself leading fifty to sixty men, just as a man can. She can give classes in politics and military strategy, and she can lead a team into combat… It's great to see women commanders exercising their authority.'[31] Nevertheless, the FARC's Secretariat has yet to contain a female member. The reason, according to one female guerrilla, is that women have only become numerically significant in the guerrilla group over the past two decades and therefore tend to have much less seniority and experience than long-time male rebels. The FARC claims that women do, however, constitute 40 per cent of mid-level commanders because increasing numbers are working their way up through the ranks.[32]

In addition to seeking empowerment, according to a 2010 report by the Washington DC-based Council on Hemispheric Affairs,

> Women also turn to the FARC to escape domestic abuse, boredom at home, and exploitation by their parents. Besides providing food and shelter, the rebel group is likely to give Colombian women new skills and a sense of self-confidence. Women in the group may feel empowered by their liberation as a result of their elevated status. Joining the FARC becomes an act of protest, a statement against the lifestyle they otherwise would have been forced to accept. It is an alternative way of life for Colombian women, one that seems very

appealing against the backdrop of abuse and hopelessness.... Moreover, other Colombian paramilitary groups are known for raping, murdering, and mutilating women, all of which the FARC offers protection from. The FARC has a zero tolerance policy towards rape and executes men who commit the act, providing a relative sense of security to female members.[33]

Guerrillas are permitted to enter into intimate relationships with each other, but have to obtain permission from their commander first. This protocol is similar to that in the US military, where soldiers posted overseas must obtain the permission of their commanding officer before getting married. FARC guerrillas also need to obtain permission to end a relationship, although it is rarely denied. Guerrilla couples engaged in relationships share a bivouac that contains a double bed. The fact that rebel fighters are frequently rotated in and out of different units makes it difficult to maintain long-term relationships. Because guerrillas are not permitted to engage in activities that interfere with their commitments as a fighter, couples are obliged to use contraception in order to avoid pregnancy. If a female guerrilla becomes pregnant, then she either has to have an abortion or turn the newborn baby over to a family member to be raised in the civilian world. Such was the case with a guerrilla named Lucero, who became pregnant and returned home to have the child. Her 8-year-old daughter was being raised by her mother and Lucero explained, 'It's hard to be away from my daughter. But I hope she talks to her grandmother and learns that her mother is a strong woman; that she understands why her mother and father are guerrillas.'[34]

Each FARC unit has a medic in its ranks to address minor wounds and illnesses. When asked what happens when a guerrilla is seriously ill or wounded, one rebel explained: 'Then the person is transported to one of the FARC's jungle hospitals, which are staffed by actual doctors. For security reasons, it is preferred that they do not go on such a journey unless it is absolutely necessary.'[35] The FARC has its own well-equipped hospitals scattered throughout the jungles of Colombia where doctors take care of seriously wounded and sick guerrillas. The hospitals also often provide medical treatment to the local civilian population. As one doctor working in a FARC hospital in Caquetá stated, 'I can do everything but brain surgery here.'[36] In February 2010, the Colombian army located and destroyed a FARC hospital in the eastern department of Guaviare that contained sixteen rooms and an electrical generator.[37]

For the most part, FARC fighters have their basic needs met, receive an education and health care, and often discover a sense of purpose – if they did not already have one when they joined. At the same time, however, guerrilla life is also rife with danger. In addition to the obvious risks posed by combat, there are the harsh physical demands of living in the jungle for years and the corresponding risk of contracting serious tropical diseases. But for those who tire of the guerrilla life, or lose their belief in the FARC, the greatest danger lies in attempting to violate the guerrilla group's requirement that its fighters be committed to the revolutionary struggle for life. In the FARC, desertion is punishable by death. Many guerrillas, however, have remained committed to their revolutionary cause. In 2007, Gladys Marín, who joined the FARC in the mid-1970s, was asked how she stayed motivated after so many years, and she responded: 'I still believe in what we're fighting for, in the revolution, in a just Colombia for everyone.'[38]

The FARC has engaged in a variety of social and economic projects, particularly in its rural strongholds. It has sought to alleviate the economic suffering of peasants, who have long been neglected by the national government. Such projects have built allegiance among the population to the rebel group in FARC-

controlled regions, where many peasants view joining the guerrillas as the only viable alternative to government repression and
social and economic neglect. Ultimately, as long as the government continues to ignore the social and economic plight of the
rural population and the FARC fills the void, then the rebel group
will maintain a base of support.

CHAPTER 4

The FARC and the Drug Trade

THE FARC's increased military strength and expanded territorial control in rural regions during the 1980s and 1990s was fuelled by several factors. Among these were the cocaine boom in the United States, an intensification of the forced displacement of peasants by paramilitaries, and the implementation of neoliberal, or so-called free-market, economic policies, which exacerbated the hardships already being endured by poor Colombians. When cocaine production exploded during the 1980s, it impacted on virtually every sector of Colombian society. The FARC was no exception, as its increasing involvement in the illicit drug trade posed distinct challenges to its ideological struggle and eventually led to it becoming the principal target in Washington's war on drugs.

North America's growing appetite for cocaine in the late 1970s allowed Pablo Escobar's Medellín drug cartel to evolve into a powerful and enormously wealthy crime syndicate, leading *Forbes* magazine to list the drug baron as the seventh richest man in the world. Escobar gained popularity among impoverished urban Colombians, especially in Medellín, by building houses and schools in poor neighbourhoods neglected by Colombian politicians. In 1982, Escobar's popularity with Medellín's lower classes led to his election as a Liberal Party alternate (deputy) to the national Congress. At the same time, Escobar and other drug traffickers were investing much of their ill-gotten wealth in vast tracts of land, particularly cattle ranches, thereby situating them firmly in the ranks of the FARC's traditional enemy.

The FARC responded by kidnapping family members of drug traffickers who refused to pay the 'war tax' that the guerrilla group levied on wealthy Colombians. Drug barons affiliated with both the Medellín and Cali cartels then responded to the kidnappings by forming paramilitary groups to defend their vast landholdings from the guerrilla threat and to target suspected rebel sympathizers. Right-wing paramilitary groups terrorized and displaced entire populations, particularly in northern Colombia, as they orchestrated an aggressive counter-agrarian reform campaign. These tactics allowed narco-landowners to increase further the size of their land holdings, while at the same time disrupting bases of peasant support for the guerrillas. By the end of the 1980s, drug traffickers had become the largest landowners in the country and, as a result, had turned much of Colombia's arable land into unproductive cattle ranches.[1]

The War on Drugs

By the early 1980s, the United States was becoming increasingly concerned about the flow of cocaine to its cities and began focusing on the Medellín cartel as the principal target in its war on drugs. In September 1984, Washington pressured the Colombian government into issuing an arrest warrant for Escobar. The drug lord responded by declaring war on the state and initiating a campaign of murder and intimidation against government officials.

What Escobar and his fellow traffickers feared most was extradition to the United States, evidenced by their slogan, 'Better a grave in Colombia than a jail cell in the United States'.

Colombia's drug traffickers turned their paramilitary forces against urban population centres in an effort to force the government to end the process of extradition. By the end of the 1980s, the government could no longer ignore the gruesome statistics: a dramatic increase in political killings from 1,053 victims per year in the 1970s to 12,859 in the 1980s.[2] President Virgilio Barco issued a rare criticism of the paramilitaries in an April 1989 address when he stated: 'The majority of their victims are not guerrillas. They are men, women, and even children, who have not taken up arms against institutions. They are peaceful Colombians.'[3] The following month, the Colombian Supreme Court ruled that Law 48, which permitted the military to organize paramilitary groups, was unconstitutional. The following month, President Barco issued Decree 1194, which made it illegal for civilians or members of the military to create, aid or participate in 'self-defence' groups.

Escobar and his associates responded by escalating their violent campaign with the intention of forcing the nation's political leaders into negotiating a peace agreement between the government and the traffickers. The cartel's leaders, calling themselves the 'Extraditables', launched a wave of urban bombing that terrorized the nation. Between 1989 and 1993, some forty car bombs killed more than 500 people, and the 1989 bombing of an Avianca airliner en route from Bogotá to Cali killed 119 passengers and crew.[4]

The introduction of the country's new constitution in 1991, which prohibited the extradition of Colombian citizens, opened the door to negotiations between Escobar and the government. That same year, Escobar reached an agreement with the government requiring that he end the violence and cease all drug trafficking activities in return for a lenient sentence to be served in a luxurious, custom-built Colombian prison. But in July 1992, Escobar fled his prison, igniting an enormous manhunt that resulted in the assassination of many of his associates. For sixteen months, US intelligence agencies, Colombian law enforcement and the rival Cali cartel worked together to track down the leader of the rapidly crumbing Medellín cartel. Finally, in December 1993, state security forces gunned down Escobar on a Medellín rooftop.

Following Escobar's death, Colombia's cocaine production and trafficking continued unabated, and the focus of US drug warriors turned to the Cali cartel, Colombia's new dominant trafficking organization. Unlike Escobar, Cali's leaders kept a low profile and used their drug profits to discreetly buy influence with many of Colombia's politicians, including President Ernesto Samper. Nevertheless, the sheer size and scope of the Cali cartel's operations left it vulnerable, and in the mid-1990s it was essentially decapitated when many of its leaders were arrested. Signally, this drug war 'victory' also failed to slow the flow of cocaine to the United States.

The demise of the Cali cartel resulted in a de-monopolization of the illicit drug industry, with dozens of micro-cartels becoming involved in the Colombian cocaine trade. Unlike the Medellín and Cali cartels, which controlled much of the cocaine trade, from processing to trafficking to distribution to US cities, the new drug lords outsourced many of their operations. They contracted individuals to pick up coca leaves or opium latex – used to produce heroin – and deliver them to processing labs. They used independent 'mules' and groups to ship the drugs northward, often to Mexico, where local gangs handled the distribution of cocaine and heroin to the United States. As a result, it has become much more difficult for US law enforcement agencies to infiltrate the new cartels. This shift in the drug trade also empowered

Mexican criminal organizations and led to a dramatic increase in drug-related violence in that country.

Each victory over Colombia's drug traffickers resulted in the emergence of new, more efficient and increasingly obscure organizations. A similar sort of balloon effect – squeezing the drug trade in one place results in expansion elsewhere – was occurring simultaneously as a result of the 'successful' coca eradication operations in Bolivia and Peru. Up until the mid-1990s, those two South American nations were the principal cultivators of coca. The Medellín and Cali cartels purchased raw coca leaves or coca paste from growers in Bolivia and Peru and then transported them to Colombia for processing into cocaine. But by the end of the 1990s, much of the region's coca cultivation had shifted to Colombia, where it doubled between 1995 and 2000.[5] The combination of intensified US-sponsored eradication campaigns in Peru and Bolivia, economic hardships due to the implementation of neoliberalism in Colombia, and an increased concentration of land ownership resulting from paramilitary operations forcibly displacing peasants to the country's frontier regions created the conditions that led to increased coca cultivation in Colombia. Much of that cultivation occurred in areas of southern and eastern Colombia controlled by the FARC, and this shift had a significant impact on the guerrilla group.

The Coca Boom

The FARC was concerned that the migration of people to the countryside and the emergence of coca in the late 1970s would undermine the political and social status quo in the areas it controlled. According to Richani,

> Coca and other illicit plantations generated a reverse migration process; the unemployed migrated from cities to areas of

colonization. The sociopolitical implications of such processes have been multifaceted, affecting the social fabric of these areas whereby the relatively stable old peasant settlements of twenty or more years mix uneasily with an impetus of new migrants seeking the 'coca rush'.... The 'coca culture' lives in tension with revolutionary ideas based on self sacrifice for the cause of radical change.[6]

There are three principal stages in the processing of coca leaves into cocaine. The first step is often done by the coca farmers themselves and involves harvesting and crushing the leaves before mixing them with sodium bicarbonate, gasoline and other additives to form a brown coca paste, which is approximately 40 per cent pure cocaine. Coca growers then sell the paste to drug labs, where hired labourers turn the brown coca paste into cocaine base by mixing it with sulphuric acid, potassium permanganate and other chemicals. The mixture is then drained and heated until it dries into a solid white compound, which is then broken up into small white rocks. The resulting cocaine base is 90 per cent pure cocaine. The third and final stage usually takes place in large remote jungle labs and involves processing the cocaine base into cocaine hydrochloride, or powder cocaine, which is 99 per cent pure. Sometimes the second and third stages of production will occur in the same lab. Traffickers then ship the cocaine hydrochloride to drug dealers in North America and Europe or to intermediaries such as the Mexican cartels.

In the early years of the cocaine boom, the FARC and the drug traffickers formed an uneasy alliance. The FARC taxed the drug traffickers and their drug production operations while ensuring that coca farmers were paid with cash and not with *bazuco* – an addictive derivative of coca paste.[7] The drug traffickers initially tolerated the taxes they had to pay to the FARC because they could not compete with the military strength of the guerrillas in coca-growing regions. But as they increasingly invested their wealth in land, they formed paramilitary groups, not only to defend themselves against guerrilla threats, but also to challenge the rebels militarily in an effort to gain control over coca-cultivating zones. By the early 1980s, the guerrillas and the drug traffickers had become arch enemies.

Throughout the 1980s and into the 1990s, despite the emerging paramilitary threat, the FARC consolidated its control over many of Colombia's coca-growing regions. As Richani notes, 'Coca plantations gradually became an important source for economic survival of more than 1 million poor peasants and colonos. The guerrillas in turn protected the peasants who worked in their areas of operations and influence.'[8] And by levying taxes of between 7 and 10 per cent of the market value of a kilo of coca paste, it is estimated that the FARC was earning between $60 million and $100 million annually by the early 1990s.[9] The coca trade was not the only factor contributing to the FARC's increased revenues; the guerrilla group also levied taxes on legal business enterprises, many of which benefited from the coca boom through the sale of precursor chemicals, and from the additional disposable income in the hands of peasants. While much attention has been paid to the FARC's taxation of the illicit drug trade in an effort to delegitimize the guerrillas, many analysts have ignored the fact that the guerrillas tax all – legal and illegal – economic activity in the regions under their control.

The FARC's increased revenues allowed the guerrilla group to better equip its fighters. Meanwhile, the deteriorating economic conditions outside the coca-growing regions and the dirty war being waged by the paramilitaries ensured a steady flow of recruits into its ranks. The FARC's upgrading of its military capabilities allowed it to expand dramatically its presence throughout rural Colombia. By 1998, it was estimated that the FARC's ranks had swelled to 18,000 fighters and that the guerrilla group controlled 622 of the nation's 1,071 municipalities, up from 173 in 1985.[10] While the rebel-controlled municipalities were still mostly situated in sparsely populated rural regions of Colombia, they constituted some 40 per cent of the national territory.

Most of the guerrilla-controlled territory lacked any significant state presence, and the FARC functioned as a de facto government. According to Alfredo Molano, 'The fact that the guerrillas were economically and militarily strong contributed to their position as the local power. They extended services in the areas of credit, education, health, justice, registry, public works, and ecological and cultural programs.'[11] And while many analysts simply reduced the FARC's territorial expansion to the profits the guerrilla group earned from the illicit drug trade, Molano argues that the principal engine of growth for the FARC was not its coca-related revenues, but rather the continuance of state repression and the impoverishment of the rural population:

> The guerrillas' rapprochement with coca also led to the belief that they are traffickers – narcoguerrillas. That notion is false, however. Cultivation of illegal crops was established in the colonization areas not simply because of weak army presence, but because the colonists were on the brink of ruin. And the guerrillas were in the colonized regions long before coca cultivation appeared. Their growth was due mainly to the repression unleashed against popular protest, and by the growing impoverishment of the population – not to their participation in the drug trade.[12]

Nevertheless, by the end of the 1990s, many critics of the FARC, on both the right and left, began pointing to the guerrilla group's involvement in the illicit drug trade as evidence that it was losing sight of its ideology and simply becoming a criminal organization. In 1996, Major Luis Alberto Villamarín of the Colombian army went so far as to call the FARC a 'drug cartel'.[13] While clearly not a cartel, by the late 1990s, the FARC was regulating the production of coca paste and cocaine base in many regions under its control and establishing the prices that drug traffickers were required to pay peasants for these products. In other words, the guerrillas played the role of facilitators and regulators of illicit drug production rather than that of actual producers and traffickers.

According to Oscar Jansson, a Swedish anthropologist who has conducted extensive field research on the political economy of coca in Putumayo, the FARC establishes a set price that farmers receive for a kilo of coca paste and then sets a higher price that processors – who usually work for the cartels – have to pay. Both the amount that farmers receive and the price that processors pay are higher than in areas controlled by the paramilitaries. When the FARC purchases the coca paste from the farmers and sells it to the processors at the higher price, the rebel group earns a profit that helps fund its insurgency.[14]

Although the FARC directly profits from the coca trade, it also guarantees that coca farmers receive a greater share of the profits than they would under the paramilitaries. Because paramilitaries look out for the interests of the cocaine processors, and by extension the drug traffickers, they ensure that farmers receive the lowest possible price for paste. Therefore, from the perspective of the drug traffickers, the more coca-growing territory that is controlled by the paramilitaries the better. In many cases, the traffickers and the paramilitaries are one and the same. If farmers in FARC-controlled areas are caught trying to sell their coca paste to another broker, the rebels often punish them by forcing them to leave the region. This is not a common occurrence since coca farmers make more money selling their product to the FARC and so there is little incentive to sell to another group.

According to economist Francisco E. Thoumi, the guerrillas differ from the drug traffickers in that 'the former's expenditures support mainly subversive activities and their political agenda, and the latter's lead to individual profits'.[15] There is no evidence that individual guerrilla leaders have personally enriched themselves; rather the guerrillas have used their drug-related wealth to further their ideological objectives. Thoumi also concludes that, while the FARC's revenues are partially dependent on the illicit drug trade, 'There is, however, no evidence that they have developed significant international marketing networks. In that sense, therefore, there is no guerrilla "cartel".'[16]

Only certain FARC fronts in drug-producing regions are engaged with the drug trade. Many guerrilla units operate in areas where there is no illicit drug production. And, as political scientist Russell Crandall has claimed, 'Some guerrillas are disgusted by the drug trade and view their involvement in it as a necessary but evil means in order to achieve a better end of social and political transformation.'[17] Accordingly, FARC–EP commander Simón Trinidad explained:

> We know that the campesinos grow illicit crops out of necessity. It is specifically a socio-economic situation. They are obligated to cultivate illicit crops because of a government that has neglected them for many years. We have made it clear that we will not take the food out of the mouth of the poor campesino. We will not leave them without jobs. They work with the marijuana and coca leaf because they don't have any other work. This problem is caused by the economic model of the Colombian state, and it is the state that has to fix the problem. We are the state's enemy, not their anti-narcotics police. The state has to offer people employment, honest work and social justice to improve their lives.[18]

James J. Brittain goes a step further, arguing that, rather than eroding its ideological foundation, the FARC's relationship to coca actually highlights the rebel group's commitment to Marxism–Leninism. He claims that Lenin condemned guerrilla

movements that failed to adapt to the social and economic realities of the working classes in which they were embedded.
Consequently, explains Brittain,

> After recognizing the material needs of the peasantry, coupled with
> the deteriorating rural political economy, the FARC–EP altered its
> political doctrine from the ground up, allowing, albeit under restric-
> tion, a means of subsistence through the cultivation of coca.... [T]he
> FARC–EP understands that revolution can only be implemented
> with the popular support of the people. Asserting this idea, the
> insurgency assisted those peasants who felt they must cultivate coca
> to survive. In recognition of this, *the FARC–EP does not support coca
> but it does support the class that must produce it.* This emphasizes
> two important points. First, the FARC–EP has proven to analyze
> and grow in revolutionary consciousness by supporting the needs
> of the marginalized. The second demonstrates how the insurgency
> continues to seek social change from below.[19]

Echoing Brittain's analysis, the US Army's Major Maddaloni
acknowledges,

> At first, the FARC leadership forbade the development of coca and
> marijuana as counter-revolutionary, counter to the social contract
> with the people, and viewed the illegal drugs as an elitist disease.
> They changed their minds when they realized the poor farmer, the
> FARC support base, had little choice but to grow drugs and they
> would ostracize this group with a hard line stance.[20]

In the late 1990s, while engaged in peace talks with the government of President Andrés Pastrana, the FARC participated in crop
substitution programmes. According to Klaus Nyholm, director
of the United Nations Drug Control Programme (UNDCP), the
FARC was cooperating with the UN in a $6 million alternative
crop project and that, in some regions of the country, rebel
fronts were actively discouraging farmers from planting coca.[21]
The guerrillas not only oversaw the substituting of coca plants

with alternative food crops; they also held a public conference to discuss alternative development strategies. The conference was attended by hundreds of representatives from Colombian and foreign civil society organizations and the guerrillas illustrated how such crop substitution projects could be successfully implemented. Proposals by the FARC to expand the projects were opposed by both the Colombian and US governments, who feared that they would provide legitimacy for the guerrillas.[22]

The 'Narco-Guerrillas'

While there was much debate regarding the nature of the FARC's involvement in the illicit drug trade, one fact had become very apparent to all Colombians and the US government by the end of the 1990s: the guerrillas posed a significant military threat to the Colombian state. The FARC's military strength had been bolstered in part by the proceeds the group was earning from the drug trade. Some estimates claimed the guerrilla group was earning as much as $900 million annually in the late 1990s.[23] By the end of that decade, the FARC was launching massive offensives against military bases in eastern and southern Colombia. Author Bert Ruiz, who was presented with Colombia's prestigious National Order of Merit by President Ernesto Samper, described an August 1998 attack by the FARC on the town of Miraflores in Guaviare in eastern Colombia:

> A force of 600 FARC guerrillas completely obliterated a key U.S.-financed police antinarcotics base located in the heart of a major coca-growing region. In blowing the well-fortified facility to pieces, the guerrillas killed 68 soldiers, wounded 87, and took numerous prisoners. The frightening aspect of the devastation in Miraflores was that the FARC forces were now entering battles with the complete confidence that they would win.[24]

A US Defense Intelligence Agency (DIA) report issued in November 1997 made clear that the United States was concerned by the threat posed by the guerrillas. The report concluded: 'The Colombian Armed Forces could be defeated within five years unless the country's government regains political legitimacy and its armed forces are drastically restructured.'[25] Officially, at the time, the United States was only providing aid to the Colombian military for counter-narcotics operations in accordance with congressional restrictions; it was not supposed to be providing counter-insurgency aid or training to Colombian troops. The reality on the ground, however, was very different. According to Stan Goff, a former US Army Special Forces soldier who was deployed as a military adviser to Colombia in the early 1990s:

> We were explicitly told that due to political sensitivities, any discussion of the mission to Colombia – like all missions going down from 7th Special Forces – was to be represented as part of the counter-narcotics effort. This was not a directive to clarify our mission, but to clarify how we were to represent the mission. What we conducted was counter-insurgency training.... The subject of every tactical discussion with Colombian planners was how to fight guerrillas, not drugs. The U.S. military is involving itself in a civil war.[26]

During the 1990s, the Clinton administration responded to the growing guerrilla threat by intensifying its war on drugs in Colombia and shifting its sights away from the drug-trafficking cartels and towards the FARC – and peasant coca growers in rebel-controlled regions. By labelling FARC members 'narco-guerrillas', the Clinton administration used the war on drugs to justify the escalation of its military intervention in Colombia's civil war.

In reality, no substantiated evidence existed to support claims that the FARC was an international drug-trafficking organization. At the time, even Donnie Marshall, chief of operations of the US

Drug Enforcement Administration (DEA), denied in testimony before Congress that the FARC was involved in drug trafficking. According to Marshall:

> The FARC factions continue to raise funds through extortion, by providing security services to traffickers, and charging a fee for each gallon of precursor chemicals and each kilo of coca leaf and cocaine HCL moving in their region.... To date, there is little to indicate the insurgent groups are trafficking in cocaine themselves, either by producing cocaine HCL and selling it to Mexican syndicates, or by establishing their own distribution networks in the United States.[27]

Nevertheless, the US State Department persisted with its claims that the FARC was nothing more than a criminal organization engaged in drug trafficking. As Colombia expert Winifred Tate noted:

> U.S. State Department officials have used arrests of individuals allegedly linked with FARC in Mexico and Brazil to bolster their claims that FARC members are 'narcoguerrillas' and to imply a complete integration of Colombia's drug cartels and guerrillas. However, these arrests involve trading of weapons for illicit drugs, and there is no evidence that FARC and other insurgent groups are seriously involved in the illicit industry's most lucrative stages: transshipment and sale of drugs on the international market.[28]

Similarly, the United Nations' special envoy to Colombia, James LeMoyne, warned in 2003 that, in a country where the inequitable wealth distribution has left 64 per cent of the population living in poverty, it would be 'a mistake to think that the FARC members are only drug traffickers and terrorists'.[29]

Under the administration of President George W. Bush, the rhetoric of the DEA shifted and it began referring to members of the FARC as drug traffickers. However, as late as 2006, the DEA seemingly contradicted its new assertions when it stated:

In general, most FARC units involved in the drug trade have remained in the lower levels, such as production and internal Colombian transportation rather than moving up to command and control or international wholesale distribution activities. The FARC, however, exerts a great deal of control over the production and distribution of cocaine in the southeastern half of Colombia.[30]

Only one week after the DEA issued that description of the FARC's limited role in drug trafficking, US attorney general Alberto Gonzales announced the indictment of fifty of the guerrilla group's top leaders on drug-trafficking charges. While the indictment accuses the FARC of operating cocaine laboratories, it does not accuse the rebel group of the actual trafficking of drugs overseas and into the United States.[31] The FARC itself continued to deny any involvement in international cocaine trafficking. But in 2004, FARC commander Trinidad was arrested in Ecuador while trying to organize negotiations for a prisoner exchange between the guerrilla group and the Colombian government. He was handed over to Colombian authorities who then extradited him to the United States to stand trial on drug-trafficking and kidnapping charges. Although Trinidad was not a member of the FARC's Secretariat, he was the highest-ranking member of the guerrilla group ever to be captured.

Trinidad was emblematic of a second generation of FARC commanders that primarily consisted of urban intellectuals who had taken up arms in the 1980s during the slaughter of the UP. Trinidad grew up in a wealthy landowning family and obtained a university degree in economics. After a short stint working in a bank he began teaching at the University of Cesar in the northern city of Valledupar. In the early 1980s, he and several other professors at the university became active in a fledgling leftist political party called Common Cause. Trinidad and his associates worked with the poor in Valledupar's barrios until the army arrested the group and accused them of being guerrillas. After his release, Trinidad became active in the UP and later avoided the slaughter of the party's members by fleeing into the jungle to join the FARC. Trinidad's role in the FARC primarily consisted of providing political and economic education as well as acting as negotiator during peace talks with the government.

In October 2007, a US judge declared a mistrial in Trinidad's drug-trafficking case due to a hung jury. The majority of the twelve jurors favoured acquittal, believing that US prosecutors had failed to prove Trinidad was involved in drug trafficking. Six months later, US prosecutors again failed to convict Trinidad of drug trafficking when another mistrial was declared, also the result of a hung jury. In a separate trial, Trinidad was convicted on kidnapping charges and sentenced to sixty years in prison. The FARC commander refused to engage in a plea bargain with US prosecutors in order to receive a reduced sentence and has remained committed to the FARC during his years in prison.

Meanwhile, a lower-level FARC fighter, Anayibe Rojas Valderama, who went by the *nom de guerre* Sonia, was also extradited to the United States to stand trial on drug-trafficking charges. Sonia was a member of the FARC's 14th Front, based in the jungles of Caquetá in southern Colombia. Prosecutors claimed that she managed the Front's finances and oversaw the production and shipping of cocaine from the region. The US government finally got its much-desired conviction of a FARC member on drug-trafficking charges in February 2007 and Sonia was sentenced to more than sixteen years in federal prison. As lawyer Paul Wolf, who observed the trials of both Trinidad and Sonia, noted, 'From now on, those on the right can refer to this case as proof that the FARC not only tax the drug trade in Colombia, but also control it. The problem is that the evidence presented consisted largely of paid government informant testimony.'[32]

According to Wolf, both Trinidad and Sonia were refused the right to retain private lawyers and were forced to accept court-appointed attorneys. Wolf noted that in Sonia's case,

> her attorney called no witnesses, had a minimal understanding of the context of the case, and could not effectively cross-examine the prosecution's witnesses.... In contrast, the prosecution had the full weight of the US and Colombian governments behind it – including numerous police and military officers, half a dozen paid informants, and thousands of documents and recorded telephone calls.[33]

The USA obtained its first drug-trafficking conviction against a FARC member even though, as Wolf notes, 'There was no physical evidence against Sonia, such as seized cocaine, fingerprints, photos, or even telephone calls that clearly referred to drugs.'[34]

In 2010, four more FARC members stood trial in the United States on drug-trafficking charges. Two pleaded guilty and two were convicted of 'conspiring to import ton-quantities of cocaine into the United States'.[35] In each case, the FARC's role in trafficking was limited to the production of cocaine in Colombia and not the actual shipping of drugs overseas.

While the FARC is undisputedly a link in the cocaine chain – as is everyone from peasant coca growers in Colombia to street dealers in the United States – US prosecutors have still yet to establish that the FARC itself is an organization that traffics cocaine internationally. As one former FARC guerrilla explains, 'The FARC controls the production of cocaine but sells it to civilian drug traffickers.'[36] And if the FARC is engaged in the international trafficking of cocaine, then it appears to be on a very small scale and to criminal networks in neighbouring Latin American nations in exchange for weapons.

If the FARC is, as many have claimed, nothing more than 'simply another Colombian drug smuggling organization' whose leaders are 'motivated by wealth and the power associated with the tens of millions earned a year from exporting cocaine', then it should be considered a failure from a criminal perspective.[37] And if FARC commanders such as Raúl Reyes are little more than the heads of a criminal organization, then they too must be considered dismal failures. After all, most Colombians who have controlled large criminal enterprises have lived in luxury. The leader of the former Medellín cocaine cartel Pablo Escobar, for example, lived lavishly in magnificent mansions and on expansive ranches, as have many other successful Colombian drug traffickers over the past thirty years. Paramilitary leaders have also lived luxuriously on their vast cattle ranches in northern Colombia, enjoying the riches wrought from their criminal activities.

In sharp contrast, there is no evidence that FARC leaders have benefited personally from the guerrilla group's financial wealth. Their life consists of sleeping on wooden planks, bathing in rivers, fighting off tropical diseases, and constantly moving through the jungle from primitive camp to primitive camp to elude US intelligence-gathering efforts and the Colombian army. The FARC's supreme commander Marulanda lived in this manner for almost half a century. Rebel commander Reyes lived in the jungle for twenty-six years with few material comforts or luxuries. After joining the Colombian Communist Party at 16 years of age, Reyes worked at a Nestlé dairy plant in Caquetá and eventually became a union leader. Disenchanted with the prospects for improving life for workers and peasants through peaceful means, he abandoned his job and headed into the jungle. The austere lifestyles of Marulanda and Reyes are hardly those of successful criminals whose principal objective is the attainment of wealth.

But while the FARC's high-ranking leaders live austere lives and have remained ideologically committed, the guerrilla group's growth in numbers and its dramatic increase in wealth have presented challenges. An examination of thousands of internal

FARC documents found on dozens of computers captured by the Colombian military show numerous instances of mid-level commanders abusing their power and misusing the rebel group's funds in order to acquire prostitutes and to purchase luxury items. The documents also show that members of the Secretariat, upon discovering the excesses, were quick to discipline those responsible. The dramatic increase in recruits during the 1990s made the FARC a potent military threat, but the new guerrilla recruits and lower-level commanders were not receiving the same degree of political and ideological indoctrination as the previous generation. Secretariat member Iván Ríos lamented the increasing loss of discipline among the ranks of the growing guerrilla army in an email he sent to his fellow Secretariat members:

> Our Achilles heel is the poor training of middle managers and even members of staffs on the fronts.... The relations between the commanders themselves and between them and the guerrillas should be redefined. It looks like laziness, *compinchería*, pandering, cronyism. We must promote a renewal and make an effort to incorporate new people.[38]

So while the illicit drug trade contributed to the FARC's increased military strength during the 1990s, the rebel group's rapid growth undermined the ideological cohesion in its ranks. The FARC needed another opportunity to refocus the country's attention on the rebel group's political objectives and to show the world that they were not simply 'narco-guerrillas'. That opportunity arrived with the election of President Andrés Pastrana in 1998.

CHAPTER 5

From 'Narco-guerrillas'
to 'Narco-terrorists'

In June 1998, Conservative Party candidate Andrés Pastrana won Colombia's presidential election by campaigning on a platform of peace. His message resonated with millions of Colombians tired of the escalating violence. Newspaper photographs during the campaign showed Pastrana meeting with the FARC's supreme commander Marulanda, leading many to believe that he could successfully negotiate a peace agreement with the guerrillas. Five months after his election, President Pastrana withdrew 2,000 soldiers and police from a 16,200 square mile area in southern and eastern Colombia known as the *zona de despeje*, or cleared zone, in preparation for peace talks with the FARC. However, the talks were conducted without a ceasefire agreement, meaning hostilities between government forces and rebels continued outside the zone. For the next two-and-a-half years, government and FARC negotiators would meet in the *zona de despeje* in an effort to address the country's problems and to bring an end to the conflict. But during this process, the geopolitical context would shift dramatically as a result of the 9/11 attacks against the United States.

The peace talks got off to an inauspicious start when President Pastrana travelled to the rebel safe haven for the official launch of negotiations and Marulanda decided at the last minute not to attend the ceremony for security reasons. Even though other members of the FARC's Secretariat attended, the media coverage focused on photos of Pastrana sitting next to an empty chair and the fact that the president had been snubbed by the rebel leader. While Marulanda's decision not to attend the ceremony was a public relations disaster for the FARC, according to author Mario Murillo,

> What was lost in the hoopla after Marulanda broke his appointment with the president, however, was the fact that during that same thirty-six-hour period, more than 150 people were killed by paramilitary death squads in different parts of the country, a personal message from the AUC [paramilitary organization] that they were not happy about the highly publicized peace talks with their archenemies.[1]

Nevertheless, the peace process continued and the FARC and the Pastrana government agreed to a twelve-point agenda for the peace talks on 6 May 1999. Among the issues to be negotiated were agrarian reform, economic and social restructuring, exploitation of the country's natural resources, human rights, military reform and international relations. The country's economy, particularly the unemployment crisis, was the first topic that was addressed. Early in 2000, the government's peace commissioner and a delegation of FARC guerrillas went on a three-week tour of Sweden, Norway, Switzerland, Italy, France and Spain, where they observed and discussed the social and economic structures of Western European democracies. Following the European tour, the FARC organized a series of public assemblies in the safe haven, which allowed Colombian citizens, NGOs, unions, indigenous organizations and business groups to discuss economic and social issues with the guerrillas.

Meanwhile, the residents of San Vicente del Caguán, the de facto capital of the safe haven, quickly became accustomed to the sight of AK-47-toting rebels patrolling the streets, shopping in their stores and eating in local restaurants. Many of the townsfolk enjoyed living in the rebel zone, not necessarily because they supported the FARC but because the removal of the other armed actors had decreased the levels of violence. As one local resident noted, 'Most Colombians would love to live like this.'[2] This attitude was not only a result of the relative peacefulness, but also due to the fact that the FARC was engaged in infrastructure improvement such as paving the streets in San Vicente and constructing a new water treatment facility. However, the local Catholic priest, Father Miguel Serna, had a different view of the guerrillas. While acknowledging that the FARC did not interfere with the Church's activities, he was nevertheless concerned about the impact of the guerrilla presence on the morals of the town's youth. 'The children don't want to work, they'd rather join the FARC', he explained. 'Many children have lost their way because they hang out on street corners admiring the guerrillas. Peace isn't just about the end of violence; it's also about ending the loss of morals.'[3]

A Military Solution

The US government did not actively support the peace process. Instead, it simultaneously formulated a militaristic strategy to combat the growing threat posed by the guerrillas. In 1999, the Clinton and Pastrana administrations devised Plan Colombia, which was launched the following year. Plan Colombia marked a dramatic increase in the level of US military intervention by tripling the amount of aid to Colombia virtually overnight, thereby making the South American nation the third largest recipient of US military aid after Israel and Egypt. Plan Colombia was sold to the US Congress and the American people as a counter-narcotics initiative, but in reality its objectives were much more far-reaching.

Colombia had avoided the 'lost decade' experienced by many Latin American nations during the 1980s that saw them experience severe debt crises. As a result, Colombia was able to keep many of its protectionist policies in place during that decade while other nations throughout the region were forced to open up their natural resources, cheap labour and markets to multinational corporations and to integrate themselves more deeply into the global economy. By the end of the 1980s, however, the Colombian government desperately needed US aid to combat the wave of urban violence being carried out by the Medellín cartel.

In September 1989, US President George H.W. Bush announced the $2.2 billion Andean Initiative and welcomed Colombia's President Virgilio Barco to Washington to discuss trade initiatives for the Andean region. In a statement afterwards, Bush said the United States 'aims to encourage and support fundamental economic reform in the countries of the region on the basis of market-driven policies'.[4] The following year, Colombia's newly elected president, César Gaviria, launched *la apertura*, or the opening, which implemented the 'market-driven policies' called for by Bush. These neoliberal, or 'free-market', policies opened up Colombia's economy to an increased flow of foreign investment and goods.

In 1999, after almost a decade of neoliberal reforms, the Colombian economy experienced its worst year since the Great Depression. It took longer than most other Latin American countries, but Colombia finally reached the point of economic desperation that provided the International Monetary Fund with the leverage it needed to directly influence the implementation of neoliberalism in the country. The structural adjustment conditions laid out in a $2.7 billion IMF loan in 1999 required Colombia to further open up its economy, privatize public companies and cut social spending, bringing Colombia into the fold of the US-dominated new world economic order.

The social consequences of the neoliberal reforms implemented during the 1990s had proven devastating for millions of Colombians. By the end of the decade, the official unemployment rate had risen to almost 20 per cent and increasing numbers of those still working were forced to subsist in the ever-growing informal sector where they lacked job security, steady pay, benefits and social security. According to the World Bank, the percentage of Colombians living in poverty increased during the second half of the 1990s from 60 per cent to 64 per cent.[5]

The economic crisis drove hundreds of thousands of Colombians from urban areas to remote rebel-controlled colonized regions to cultivate coca in order to survive. Reflecting on the country's economic situation, FARC commander Raúl Reyes declared:

> The perverse designs of the neo-liberal model only result in more backwardness, dependence and underdevelopment for peoples of the continent. In the concrete case of Colombia, it has engendered greater violence, corruption and impunity, more starving and unemployed, on top of the previous calamities. On the other hand, in the absence of policies to promote domestic production, especially in agriculture, the ideologues and apostles who preach this model have definite responsibility for the proliferation of the drug traffic and all its harmful results. Therefore, policies really aimed at combating the drug traffic as a social phenomenon of the system will necessarily have to undergo a substantial revision of their economic, political, social and cultural content.[6]

Also, at the end of the 1990s, the Colombian government found itself in a predicament similar to that of a decade earlier: it was being violently attacked by a powerful organization. Only this time, it was the FARC instead of the Medellín cartel. Once again, the government turned to the United States for aid and the Clinton administration responded with Plan Colombia. The objectives of Plan Colombia were to reduce coca cultivation by 50 per cent in five years, to end the country's armed conflict by undermining the FARC's funding through the fumigation of coca crops, and to reform the economy. The IMF's loan to Colombia the previous year constituted the economic component of Plan Colombia while the military element of the US aid package – totalling more than 70 per cent of the total aid – would be used to target coca and the FARC. The FARC became the principal military target of Plan Colombia even though the paramilitaries were far more deeply engaged in drug trafficking. In 1997, the regional paramilitary groups had formed a coalition called the United Self-Defence Forces of Colombia (Autodefensas Unidas de Colombia, AUC) and three years later its leader, Carlos Castaño, publicly acknowledged that 70 per cent of the AUC's funding came from drug revenues.[7]

FARC commander Iván Ríos claimed that Plan Colombia was not just about combating cocaine, but also about advancing US economic interests in Colombia:

> Narco-trafficking is an international problem that originates in the big consuming centres. It is big business; it is immense. The second-biggest business in the capitalist world; it is bigger than the petroleum business. And it isn't Colombians who are enjoying the fruits of this business. It is the excuse that the United States uses to interfere with things here in Colombia. We want the American people to be better informed about the narco-trafficking business and the situation in Colombia and the other Andean countries. The United States wants to dominate us because we are a geopolitically important country. The United States wants to dominate Colombia to control its resources. This is the desire of the government of the United States, not of its people.[8]

During a visit to the Colombian port city of Cartagena in 1999, US energy secretary Bill Richardson clearly outlined US economic interests in the South American country when he declared: 'The United States and its allies will invest millions of dollars in two areas of the Colombian economy, in the areas of mining and energy, and to secure these investments we are tripling military aid to Colombia.'[9] Within months it became apparent that the IMF loan conditions were intended to create favourable investment terms for multinational corporations and that Plan Colombia would establish the necessary security on the ground to allow those companies to exploit the country's resources.

Plan Colombia was about more than simply combating the illicit drug trade; it was to be the mechanism through which neoliberalism would be militarily implemented in Colombia. After all, most of Colombia's abundant oil and mineral resources desired by multinational corporations were situated in rural regions where the FARC was active. Therefore IMF economic reforms alone would not prove sufficient in Colombia as they had done throughout the rest of the region.

Under Plan Colombia, US-piloted spray planes supported by US-supplied Blackhawk helicopter gunships routinely fumigated coca crops in southern and eastern Colombia, focusing primarily on the oil-rich department of Putumayo. Hundreds of thousands of hectares were fumigated, but the spraying not only destroyed coca crops, it also devastated food crops, adversely affected the health of children and displaced thousands of families.[10]

There were also widespread accusations of corruption and waste with regard to the 8 per cent of US aid earmarked for alternative crop programmes. Jair Giovani Ruiz, an agro-industrial engineer with the Ministry of the Environment's Corpoamazonia (Corporation for Sustainable Development in the Southern Amazon), claimed that peasants had received little of the alternative crop funding: 'Maybe a cow or three chickens, but the farmers can't live off of these. Maybe the money got lost on the way, or maybe [the government] contracted a lot of experts in order to supply a cow.' The bottom line, according to Ruiz, was that 'there was bad management of Plan Colombia's resources'.[11]

The more than 70 per cent of US aid that constituted Plan Colombia's military component had, however, proven very effective at destroying the livelihoods of impoverished farmers. In response, Mario Cabal of the National Plan for Alternative Development (Plan Nacional de Desarrollo Alternativo, PLANTE), the government agency in charge of the underfunded alternative crop programme, complained: 'We have money for helicopters and arms for war, but we don't have money for social programmes.'[12]

Many of the farmers who did participate in the alternative crop programme by signing social pacts that required them to voluntarily uproot their coca plants in return for $1,000 in materials, technical assistance, and a promise that they would not be fumigated, had their new crops sprayed. According to Doctor Ruben Dario Pinzón of PLANTE, 'Growers financed by PLANTE have been fumigated because they are in a small area in the middle of coca growers. It is impossible to protect them because the pilots can't control exactly where they fumigate. They fumigate the whole area.'[13] Victoriano, a farmer in Putumayo, signed a social pact with PLANTE in April 2002 and replaced his coca plants with lulo plants, which produce fruit used to make juice drinks. Four months later, his newly planted lulo crops were destroyed by aerial fumigation. Meanwhile, two nearby coca fields were scarcely affected by the herbicide. When asked what he was going to do now that his alternative crops had been killed, Victoriano replied: 'Grow coca again.'[14]

In some of the FARC's traditional strongholds, the guerrilla group constituted the only source of aid for peasants whose crops had been fumigated. Following aerial fumigations in the eastern department of Meta, a peasant woman named Cecilia explained how the family cultivated food crops for subsistence and coca to earn money to purchase other essentials. When the planes came and fumigated her small farm, the chemicals killed not only the coca crops, but also their food crops. Their small two-room wooden shack and her two small children were also coated with the chemicals, making the children sick with diarrhoea and vomiting. Afterwards, friends whose crops had survived the spraying provided Cecilia and her family with food and the FARC gave her money to purchase medicine for her sick children.[15]

Peasants who have been fumigated are often left with only two choices: displacement or replanting. Sometimes the replanting takes place on the same plots of land that were fumigated; at other times peasants cut down more rainforest. Usually, coca is the first crop that peasants replant because it produces four or five harvests a year, thereby providing them with a means of subsistence far more quickly than food crops, some of which require several seasons to produce their first yield. But as one farmer living in La Macarena National Park in the department of Meta, whose crops had been fumigated, explained, 'If you simply start cutting down trees to plant more crops, the FARC will fine you. We must obtain permission from the guerrillas before we can cut down the rainforest.'[16] It is not always easy to obtain that permission because the FARC is attempting to carry out a balancing act between funding its insurgency from coca, allowing peasants to earn a living, and limiting the destruction of one of the country's most exquisite ecological treasures.

Despite more than $4 billion in US funding during its first five years, Plan Colombia never came close to achieving its principal counter-narcotics objective of reducing coca cultivation by 50 per cent. In fact, according to statistics released by the US Office of National Drug Control Policy (ONDCP), coca cultivation in Colombia was higher in 2005 than when Plan Colombia was initiated five years earlier. Furthermore, coca cultivation had spread from six of the country's thirty-two departments at the outset of Plan Colombia to twenty-three by 2005.[17] Even though hundreds of thousands of hectares of coca had been fumigated, the price, purity and availability of cocaine in US cities remained unaffected. Despite the failure of Plan Colombia to achieve its principal stated objective, both the Bush and Obama administrations would continue it.

Meanwhile, in early 2002, the peace process had stalled. The principal problem was the deadlock between the two sides on the issue of the economy. The FARC wanted to negotiate an end to the implementation of neoliberalism, but so far as the government was concerned the economic model was non-negotiable. Sensing the growing public frustration with the oft-stalled negotiations and the FARC's kidnapping outside the safe haven of Senator Jorge Gechem Turbay, President Pastrana ended the fledgling three-year peace process at midnight on 20 February 2002. Government officials in Washington and Bogotá, as well as the mainstream media in both countries, immediately blamed the FARC for the collapse of the talks. According to US State Department spokesman James Rubin, 'The blame for the failure of the peace talks to proceed rests squarely on the shoulders of FARC leaders Manuel Marulanda and Jorge Briceño. They are personally responsible for this setback.'[18]

Pastrana used the FARC's refusal to agree to a ceasefire and its ongoing military operations and 'terrorist' activities during the negotiations as justification for ordering the Colombian military to invade the rebel safe haven. But while the FARC was repeatedly condemned for continuing to wage war outside the *zona de despeje*, few questioned the fact that the Colombian military and the paramilitaries were doing exactly the same thing. The government also criticized the FARC's use of the safe haven to increase its military strength. And again, few analysts and media outlets questioned the fact that the Colombian military was also being strengthened during the peace process due to Plan Colombia. In fact, only one week after President Clinton had announced Plan Colombia, General Charles Wilhelm, commander-in-chief of the US military's Southern Command, stated: 'While I share the widely held opinion that the ultimate solution to Colombia's internal problems lies in negotiations, I am convinced that success on the battlefield provides the leverage that is a precondition for meaningful and productive negotiations.'[19]

Throughout the negotiations, the FARC repeatedly stated that it would not agree to a ceasefire until the government dismantled the paramilitaries, who had continued waging their dirty war. The guerrilla group was not about to make the same mistake it had made in the 1980s, when more than two thousand members of the UP were slaughtered during and after the ceasefire with the Betancur government. As Raúl Reyes, the FARC's second-in-command, had explained to a US State Department official in a clandestine meeting in Costa Rica at the outset of the peace process, 'We cannot have a situation where the paramilitaries exist without checks. Therefore, there will be no peace agreement until the government does something about the paramilitaries.'[20]

The Terrorist Lens

The terrorist attacks against the United States on 11 September 2001 provided the Bush administration with an opportunity to further expand US military intervention in Colombia. Within weeks, the rhetoric emanating from both Washington and Bogotá shifted to emphasizing the US State Department's listing of the FARC as an international terrorist organization. Less than three weeks after 9/11, Democratic Senator Bob Graham of Florida, chairman of the Senate Select Committee on Intelligence, launched a campaign to portray the FARC as a major international terrorist threat:

> The FARC are doing the same thing as global level terrorists, that is organizing in small cells that don't have contact with each other and depend on a central command to organize attacks, in terms of logistics and finance. It is the same style of operation as Bin Laden.[21]

In October 2001, the State Department's top counterterrorism official, Francis X. Taylor, declared that Washington's strategy for fighting terrorism in the Western hemisphere would include, 'where appropriate, as we are doing in Afghanistan, the use of military power'.[22] Taylor left little doubt about the 'appropriate' target when he stated that the FARC 'is the most dangerous international terrorist group based in this hemisphere'.[23] Meanwhile, Taylor's boss, US Secretary of State Colin Powell, told the Senate Foreign Relations Committee that the FARC belonged in the same category as al-Qaeda: 'There is no difficulty in identifying [Osama bin Laden] as a terrorist and getting everybody to rally against him. Now, there are other organizations that probably meet a similar standard. The FARC in Colombia comes to mind.'[24]

In the last week of October, Senator Graham ramped up his accusations, declaring that Colombia should be the principal battlefield in the global war on terror. According to the Florida senator, there were almost 500 incidents of terrorism committed worldwide against US citizens and interests in 2000, and 'of those almost 500 incidents, 44 per cent were in one country. Was that country Egypt? No. Israel? No. Afghanistan? Hardly a tick.

Forty-four per cent were in Colombia. That's where the terrorist war has been raging.'[25]

What Graham failed to mention was that the overwhelming majority of 'terrorist' attacks against the United States by Colombian guerrillas consisted of bombing oil pipelines used by US companies; in other words, they were designed to hurt corporate profit margins, not US civilians. In fact, the Florida senator neglected to point out that these attacks did not kill a single US citizen in 2000, the year to which Graham was referring. Nevertheless, the propaganda campaign vilifying the FARC successfully laid the groundwork for US ambassador Anne Patterson's announcement at the end of October that the United States would provide counterterrorism aid to Colombia as part of Washington's new global war on terror.

Given the widespread public support in the United States for a global war on terror, it was no surprise that the US Congress approved a $28 billion counterterrorism bill in July 2002 that included $35 million in supplemental aid for Colombia. More important than the additional funds, however, was the fact that the new bill eliminated the conditions restricting US military aid to Colombia to counternarcotics programmes. This change allowed the military aid that had constituted more than 70 per cent of the $2 billion in Plan Colombia counternarcotics funding since 2000 – as well as future drug war funding – to be used for counter-insurgency operations as part of the war on terror.[26]

The Bush administration worked hard to link drugs to terrorism by attempting to convince the US public and Congress that the habits of illegal drug users were bankrolling terrorist groups. In June 2003, the Bush administration's propaganda campaign made the ultimate claim linking illegal drug use to terrorism when General James Hill, commander of the US Army's Southern Command, told the Senate Caucus on International Narcotics

Control that drugs were a 'weapon of mass destruction'.[27] Despite repeated assurances by US officials in 2000 that Plan Colombia did not constitute an expansion of the US military role in Colombia beyond the drug war, the mission creep that critics feared had now occurred. The line between Washington's war on drugs and Colombia's armed conflict, as thin as it was, had been completely erased.

The Democratic Security Strategy

The US military escalation under the war on terror coincided with the military solution to Colombia's conflict sought by that country's newly elected president, Alvaro Uribe. During the 2002 presidential campaign, Uribe's hard-line stance towards the guerrillas appealed to those Colombians who had become disillusioned following the failed peace process between the Pastrana administration and the FARC. The right-wing Uribe declared that he would not negotiate with the FARC or any other armed group unless they first agreed to a ceasefire. In fact, Uribe denied that an armed conflict existed in Colombia, instead claiming that the government was simply fighting 'criminal' or 'terrorist' organizations. The new Colombian president's aggressive approach also resonated with the Bush administration, which desperately wanted a hard-line ally in Bogotá.

Upon assuming office in August 2002, Uribe began implementing his Democratic Security and Defence Strategy, through which the state intended to gain control over conflict areas. Within a year, the Uribe administration achieved a dramatic 23 per cent drop in kidnappings.[28] The democratic security strategy also achieved a 16 per cent decline in homicides during the same period. However, the decrease in murders was the result of fewer common homicides; political killings remained stable. According to the Bogotá-based human rights group Colombian Commission of Jurists (Comisión Colombiana de Juristas, CCJ), 6,978 people were killed for socio-political reasons during Uribe's first year in office, which amounted to ninteen people a day, the same rate as the previous two years. The CCJ determined that paramilitaries were responsible for at least 62 per cent of the killings, more than double the amount committed by the guerrillas.[29]

While Uribe's democratic security strategy was making life safer for some Colombians, particularly those living in urban areas, it was targeting anyone who dared to criticize the government's policies. Among the many repressive actions undertaken in the name of democratic security was the rounding up of more than two thousand residents in the town of Saravena in the eastern department of Arauca. The mass arrests by the Colombian military took place during the night of 12 November 2002 and, according to Amnesty International,

> By the end of the night more than 2,000 people had been rounded up at gunpoint and taken to Saravena's stadium where they were photographed, videotaped, questioned, their background checked, and their arms marked with indelible ink.... Most of Saravena's human rights community, as well as many known trade unionists and other social leaders were among the 2,000 people detained that night.[30]

There were numerous other instances of mass arbitrary arrests perpetrated by state security forces. On 24 August 2003, some 600 soldiers and police raided homes in Cajamarca in central Colombia and arrested 56 people. Among those detained were an elderly paraplegic and the local priest. The same month, 128 people were arrested in the north-western city of Sincelejo for alleged ties to the FARC. They were all imprisoned for three months before being released due to a lack of evidence.[31] During Uribe's first year in office, according to the CCJ, 4,362 people were the subject of arbitrary arrest; almost double the total for the previous six years.[32] And the Colombian human rights group José Alvear Restrepo Lawyers' Collective claimed that most of those detained were arrested 'for their social activity, or simply for living in areas that authorities consider "suspect"'.[33]

Also during Uribe's first year in office, 3,593 people were 'disappeared', according to the Association of Family Members of the Detained and Disappeared (ASFADDES), a Colombian NGO. This number represented a dramatic increase over the 3,413 people who were disappeared between 1994 and 2001.[34] In a trend eerily reminiscent of the dirty war in Argentina and other Southern Cone countries, paramilitaries and state security forces were responsible for a huge majority of the disappearances, according to the United Nations.[35] As Gloria Gómez of ASFADDES noted, 'In Argentina, their tragedy happened in a short space of time, and the image of the junta in their military uniforms made it easy to generate international antipathy. Our authoritarianism wears a suit and tie and was democratically elected.'[36]

On 8 September 2003, Uribe launched a verbal attack against NGOs during a nationally televised speech at a military ceremony in Bogotá. During his speech, the president accused human rights groups of being terrorists. The accusations were made in response to a 172-page report issued earlier that day by a coalition of eighty NGOs criticizing the president's security policies. The NGO report claimed that the human rights situation had worsened under Uribe because of 'indiscriminate military operations' that sought to achieve 'social control and to implant terror in the population'. As a result, according to the report, the number of people whose human rights were violated due to extrajudicial executions, forced disappearances, torture and arbitrary detentions had increased dramatically during Uribe's first year in office.[37]

During his speech, in what was clearly a reference to the eighty organizations that issued the report, Uribe claimed there was a group of NGOs that were 'politicking at the service of terrorism'. He went on to say that the NGOs 'cowardly shield themselves behind the human rights banner to try to give back to terrorism the space that public forces and citizens have taken from them'. The president then directly linked human rights groups to the guerrillas when he stated: 'Every time a security policy is carried out in Colombia to defeat terrorism, when terrorists start feeling weak, they immediately send their spokesmen to talk about human rights.'[38]

Three weeks after his verbal attack on NGOs, Uribe visited the United States where he spoke at the United Nations and met with US Secretary of State Colin Powell. Not only did Powell fail to criticize the Colombian leader for his recent verbal tirade against human rights defenders, he actually affirmed the US government's support for Uribe. Following the Colombian president's claims at the UN that his government respected the work of human rights groups, Powell said he was impressed by Uribe's 'clear commitment to human rights in the prosecution of this war that he is fighting against terrorists and against drug lords in Colombia'.[39]

Uribe's accusations against NGOs did more than illustrate the Colombian president's attitude towards human rights; it endangered the lives of human rights workers. Right-wing paramilitaries, who also view human rights defenders as guerrilla sympathizers, likely perceived Uribe's message to be a 'green light' for targeting NGO workers. The symmetry between Uribe's attitudes towards NGOs and that of the paramilitaries was clearly evident in comments made by an AUC paramilitary commander in Putumayo: 'It is not a secret that the NGOs are managed by guerrillas. NGOs are giving money to certain people so they'll make claims against army generals.... The NGOs are managed by the subversives.'[40]

Right-wingers such as President Uribe claimed that the FARC has no popular support, often referring to notoriously inaccurate opinion polls in which the guerrilla group usually received a 2 per cent approval rating while Uribe garnered absurdly high levels of support – in the 70 to 80 per cent range. The overwhelming majority of polls, however, are conducted by telephone in the country's four largest cities. Inevitably, the views of middle- and upper-class urban residents dominate the results. Furthermore, given the repressive nature of the government, it is doubtful that FARC sympathizers would openly profess their support or approval of the guerrilla group to a pollster.

So while the right claims on the one hand that the FARC has no popular support, on the other it argues that many NGOs support the guerrillas; that peasants living in regions controlled by the FARC who are targeted by the military's counter-insurgency operations are sympathetic to the rebels; that the thousands of leftist politicians, NGO workers and community leaders who have been arbitrarily arrested by the Uribe government are all 'spokespersons' for the guerrillas; that many of the country's union leaders are rebels; and that the country's universities are full of guerrilla sympathizers.

This contradictory position – that the FARC has no popular support and that widespread sectors of civil society support the guerrillas – is repeatedly voiced by the right and is rarely challenged by the mainstream media. But the right cannot have it both ways. Either the FARC has significant support among civil society groups and the peasant population or it does not. And if the FARC has no significant popular support, then all of those sectors of civil society that are routinely repressed by the government cannot be guerrilla sympathizers. In which case, there must be another reason that those sectors of the population are being targeted; and that reason is that they dare to challenge non-violently the government's security and economic policies.

Ultimately, the reality lies somewhere between the two contradictory extremes claimed by the right. There are individuals and sectors within civil society that sympathize, and even collaborate, with the guerrillas, but are forced to conceal this reality in order to survive. There are also many who do not support the guerrillas and who would argue that the continued existence of the FARC and the ELN provides the Colombian government with a convenient justification for repressing civil society organizations.

With regard to the general population, relations between local residents and the FARC differ greatly depending on the history of the region. There are three principal scenarios regarding the FARC's relationship with the civilian population. In areas where the guerrillas have maintained a presence for decades, as in much of Caquetá, Meta, Guaviare and Putumayo, as well as in parts of Huila, Tolima and Nariño, the peasants and the rebels are often organically linked – many local peasants are guerrillas, and vice versa. In rural regions of the country in which the FARC has primarily established its presence over the past twenty years, however, there is often a certain amount of distrust of the rebels among the local population. This stems from the fact that the guerrillas are not historically linked to the local peasant populations and their presence in those regions is often primarily a military one. Furthermore, there is usually also a military and paramilitary presence in those regions, which often results in the civilian population becoming caught in the middle of the conflict between the armed actors. This is especially true in many parts of northern Colombia. The third scenario involves larger towns and cities where the state has historically dominated. While the FARC may have some support in the poor urban barrios and even among certain progressive sectors of the middle class, much of the population in these areas tends to view the guerrillas as the country's principal problem.

Despite the repressive nature of Uribe's democratic security strategy and its blatant targeting of non-violent civil society groups, the Bush administration openly endorsed the Colombian government's approach. On a December 2002 visit to Bogotá, US Secretary of State Colin Powell met with Uribe and declared:

> We support your new national security strategy. It is a comprehensive plan to build a healthy democracy. A key part of that strategy, indeed, the part that makes everything else possible, is that element of the plan directed towards defeating the deadly combination of terrorism and drugs.[41]

The Oil Factor

US support for Uribe was evident not only in the rhetoric of Bush administration officials, but also in the provision of counterterrorism aid. In the same manner that the FARC's fighters were labelled 'narco-guerrillas' and became the principal target of Plan Colombia under the guise of Washington's war on drugs, the term 'narco-terrorists' was regularly applied to the rebels following 9/11 and they immediately became the principal target of the US war on terror in Colombia. And, as also had occurred with Plan Colombia, an increase in US military aid – this time counterterrorism aid – coincided with an IMF loan to Colombia. In January 2003, the IMF authorized a two-year, $2.1 billion loan to the South American nation; the same month, US Army Special Forces soldiers arrived in the oil-rich department of Arauca.

The Uribe government fulfilled the neoliberal conditions attached to the IMF loan by completing the transformation of the country's oil regime. In 1999, prior to both the first IMF loan and Plan Colombia, foreign corporations operating in Colombia's oil sector were required to enter into a 50–50 partnership with the state oil company Ecopetrol. They were also required to pay a 20 per cent royalty rate on their share of the oil extracted and obligated to give up their rights to a productive field after twenty-two years. By 2004, foreign companies no longer had to enter into partnership with Ecopetrol; they could own 100 per cent of the oil in a field to which they owned the concession. Furthermore, the royalty rate had been reduced to only 8 per cent in most cases and companies held the rights to the oil for the life of the field.[42]

But while IMF economic reforms had created favourable investment conditions for multinational oil companies, there still existed the problem of security on the ground. Many of Colombia's oil reserves were situated in rural regions dominated by the guerrillas. Plan Colombia had provided security for companies operating in oil-rich Putumayo in southern Colombia, which was also a principal coca-growing region. The implementation of Plan Colombia in Putumayo had followed on the heels of a dramatic increase in the number of attacks against the department's oil infrastructure from 48 in 1999 to 110 the following year. The growing military strength of the FARC in Putumayo during the 1990s had made foreign oil companies hesitant to exploit the vast oil reserves that mostly existed in rebel-controlled regions.

The situation changed with the arrival of AUC paramilitaries in the late 1990s and the implementation of Plan Colombia in 2000, both of which resulted in greater security for oil operations. According to the Colombian army commander responsible for protecting Putumayo's oil operations, Lieutenant Colonel Francisco Javier Cruz, US drug war aid made the region safer for conducting oil operations because the army was able to use 'helicopters, troops and training provided in large part by Plan

Colombia'.[43] Since 2004, the Colombian government has signed dozens of contracts with foreign oil companies providing them with the rights to exploit the oil in Putumayo. And Lt. Col. Cruz is clear regarding the mission of his troops: 'Security is the most important thing to me. Oil companies need to work without worrying and international investors need to feel calm.'[44]

Because the US Congress had restricted the use of Plan Colombia's military funding to operations in drug-producing regions such as Putumayo, oil companies operating in the oil-rich department of Arauca in eastern Colombia did not benefit from the military escalation. Consequently, in 2001, FARC and ELN guerrillas demanding that the government fully nationalize the oil industry bombed the Caño Limón oil pipeline a record 170 times, shutting it down for 240 days during the year and costing Los Angeles-based Occidental Petroleum $100 million in lost earnings.[45]

The Bush administration's war on terror provided the opportunity for an expansion of US military intervention in Colombia into areas devoid of coca crops and other illicit drug production activities; areas such as Arauca. In 2002, Congress approved $93 million in counterterrorism aid for the protection of the pipeline. With the aid package, US taxpayers began paying $3.55 in security costs for every barrel of Occidental oil that flowed through the pipeline. This figure contrasted sharply with the 50 cents per barrel that the company was contributing to its own security costs.[46] With a war in Iraq looming on the horizon and instability in Venezuela, Colombia had become an important alternative source of oil. Colombia was already among the top suppliers of oil to the United States when, following 9/11, US ambassador to Colombia Anne Patterson stated: 'Colombia has the potential to export more oil to the United States, and now more than ever, it's important for us to diversify our sources of oil.'[47]

In January 2003, 70 US Army Special Forces soldiers – 30 based in the departmental capital, Arauca City, and 40 in the town of Saravena – were deployed to a region that had long been under the influence of the FARC and the ELN. The US soldiers provided counter-insurgency training to units of the Colombian army's 18th Brigade, teaching Colombian troops how to conduct reconnaissance missions and wage unconventional warfare, among other things. The insignia of the 18th Brigade includes an oil derrick, and its commander, Brigadier General Carlos Lemus, directed operations from an office inundated with souvenirs bearing the name of the company whose oil it was his mission to protect. Occidental Petroleum contributes both money and logistical support, including transport helicopters, to the 18th Brigade to assist with protection of the pipeline. General Lemus explained the need for the US military aid and training: 'We need some of these things to help protect the pipeline and provide troop mobility, training, and more intelligence capacity to allow our troops to be able to respond to attacks more efficiently and faster.'[48]

The new US counter-insurgency role meant that US soldiers were working with Colombian troops closely allied with para-militaries responsible for gross violations of human rights. In 2001, AUC paramilitaries were responsible for 70 per cent of the more than 420 political killings – including the assassinations of two local congressmen – in the vicinity of Arauca City.[49] While General Lemus denied any links between his troops and paramilitaries, Amnesty International claimed to have 'received information indicating strong collusion between units of the 18th Brigade of the Colombian army and paramilitaries, including reports of joint military–paramilitary operations or army units wearing paramilitary armbands and identifying themselves as paramilitaries'.[50]

In one such operation in May 2003, paramilitaries and soldiers from the 18th Brigade entered the Betoyes indigenous reserve in the municipality of Tame as part of an offensive called Operation Colosso. The gunmen raped and killed a pregnant 16-year-old indigenous girl and then cut the foetus out of her stomach before disposing of her body in a river.[51] When asked about the paramilitary strategy of entering villages and massacring unarmed civilians accused of being guerrilla collaborators, one US Army Special Forces soldier based in Saravena replied, 'Sometimes that's what you have to do, I guess.'[52]

The Colombian army's 18th Brigade has also used its newly acquired unconventional warfare skills against civilians critical of the government's policies. During 2003, while the US military advisers were stationed in Arauca, there were numerous mass arrests of union leaders, human rights defenders and opposition politicians who were accused of maintaining ties to 'terrorist' groups, namely the guerrillas. On 21 August in Saravena, soldiers from the 18th Brigade raided homes and arrested forty-two trade unionists, social activists and human rights defenders. Among those arrested and accused of being 'subversives' was José Murillo, president of the Joel Sierra Regional Human Rights Committee. Murillo had recently criticized the collusion between the Colombian army and paramilitaries in Saravena.[53] The arrests were carried out by Colombian soldiers from the same base that housed the US Army Special Forces troops.

In October 2003, soldiers from the Colombian army's 18th Brigade rounded up more than twenty-five politicians in Arauca less than a week before local elections. Among those arrested for suspected ties to the guerrillas were the mayor of Arauca City, the president of the regional assembly, a candidate for governor, and five mayoral candidates. Defence Minister Marta Lucía Ramírez explained the arrests: 'Unfortunately, terrorist groups have infiltrated the Department of Arauca at every level.'[54] But Amnesty International accused the Uribe administration of politicizing human rights, claiming, 'A lot of it has to do with silencing those who campaign for human and socio-economic rights.' The timing of the arrests, only days before local elections, also led an Amnesty spokesperson to declare: 'It is part of a strategy to undermine the opposition's credibility.'[55]

On 5 August 2004, Colombian soldiers from the same base housing the US military advisers again ventured out into Saravena's barrios. This time, the soldiers dragged three union leaders out of their beds in the middle of the night and executed them. The Colombian army initially claimed that the three unionists were armed guerrillas killed in battle. A high-profile investigation conducted by local and international human rights groups led to Colombia's attorney general's office opening its own investigation. One month after the killings, Deputy Attorney General Luis Alberto Santana announced: 'The evidence shows that a homicide was committed. We have ruled out that there was combat.'[56] In a rare case of justice being carried out in Colombia's dirty war, one army officer and two Colombian soldiers were arrested and charged with the murder of the three union leaders.

The deployment of US Army Special Forces troops to Arauca illustrates how 9/11 dramatically changed the political landscape, allowing the Bush administration to send US troops to one of the most conflict-ridden regions of Colombia as part of the global war on terror. The Bush administration's expansion of the US role in Colombia effectively turned US soldiers into Occidental Petroleum's personal security trainers. The efforts of the US Army Special Forces soldiers, who trained more than two thousand Colombian troops in two years, paid dividends for the US oil company as the Caño Limón pipeline was bombed only seventeen times in 2004.[57] The US advisers, however, had helped secure Occidental's operations by providing counter-insurgency training to a Colombian army brigade directly responsible for gross violations of human rights.

Terrorists or Belligerents?

Despite the egregious violations of human rights by the US-backed Colombian military, it was the FARC that was repeatedly being labelled as terrorist by the US and Colombian governments, and by the mainstream media. While there is not a universally accepted definition of terrorism, the most widely accepted definitions include three crucial components: the use or threat of violence, against civilians, for political gain. Under such a definition, both the state and sub-national groups could be considered terrorists. In the case of Colombia's conflict, all of the armed actors – military, paramilitaries and guerrillas – have repeatedly perpetrated acts of terrorism according to this definition. But according to the US State Department, 'The term "terrorism" means premeditated, politically motivated violence perpetrated against noncombatant targets by subnational groups or clandestine agents, usually intended to influence an audience.'[58] There is no allowance under this definition for state terrorism, such as that routinely perpetrated by the Colombian military.

The State Department does, however, list state sponsors of terrorism, claiming that 'State sponsors of terrorism provide critical support to many non-state terrorist groups.'[59] However, despite the Colombian military's well-documented collusion with a paramilitary organization on the US State Department's list of terrorist groups, Colombia has never been listed as a state sponsor of terrorism.

Noam Chomsky has argued that these sorts of contradictions make evident that the terrorist label is a political weapon rather than an accurate description of an armed actor in any particular conflict. In other words, it is 'terrorism' when the United States or its allies are attacked, but when the United States or its allies perpetrate a similar form of violence then it is 'self-defence' or 'humanitarian intervention', and the dead civilians are casually dismissed as 'collateral damage'.[60] Other prominent figures have also criticized the labelling of the FARC as a terrorist organization in order to present the guerrillas as little more than criminals. The UN's special envoy to Colombia, James LeMoyne, has argued, 'Despite the methods the group uses, it's an error to think that FARC are just terrorists as the Colombian government calls them or narco-traffickers because the backbone of the guerrilla movement consists of persons ideologically committed.[61]

Not surprisingly, the FARC has rejected the terrorist label; in fact the guerrilla group has argued that it deserves to have 'belligerent' status bestowed upon it, which formalizes the rights and duties of all armed actors in a war under the Geneva Conventions. According to lawyer Paul Wolf,

> For a state of belligerency to be recognized, it is necessary that (1) the insurgents occupy a certain part of the State territory; (2) establish a government exercising the rights inherent in sovereignty on that part of territory; and (3) conduct the hostilities by organized troops kept under military discipline and complying with the laws and customs of war.[62]

Wolf argues that the FARC clearly fulfils the requirements for belligerent status:

> The FARC–EP are a belligerent army of national liberation, as evidenced by their sustained military campaign and sovereignty over a large part of Colombian territory, and their conduct of hostilities by organized troops kept under military discipline and complying with the laws and customs of war, at least to the same extent as

other parties to the conflict. Members of the FARC–EP are therefore entitled to the rights of belligerents under international law.[63]

In January 2008, Venezuela's National Assembly voted in favour of supporting President Hugo Chávez's call for the Colombian government to bestow belligerent status upon both the FARC and the ELN. Chávez argued that belligerent status would open the door to negotiations and force the guerrillas to abide by the Geneva Conventions with regard to kidnapping and acts of terrorism.[64] Chávez also called on the European Union to remove both Colombian guerrilla groups from its list of terrorist organizations, and in reference to the FARC declared, 'They're a real army that occupies territory in Colombia, they're not terrorists. They have a political goal and we have to recognize that.'[65]

As is to be expected, given Chávez's leftist leanings, Colombian and US officials have repeatedly made unsubstantiated claims that the Venezuelan leader provides material support to the FARC. And in March 2008 the Bush administration launched a legal review of Venezuela to determine if the country should be placed on the State Department's list of state sponsors of terrorism. Ultimately, Venezuela was not placed on the list.[66] While such a designation would have aided the Bush administration's propaganda campaign to vilify Chávez – and the FARC – it was unlikely to happen given that such a move would have forced Washington to impose sanctions on one of the leading suppliers of oil to the United States.

The bestowing of belligerent status on the FARC by the Colombian government would require the guerrillas, as Chávez noted, to abide by the rules of war under the Geneva Conventions. It would also force the Colombian government to acknowledge a state of internal war and treat captured guerrillas as prisoners of war rather than as common criminals, thereby prohibiting the extradition of captured FARC members to the United States. The Colombian government has little interest in providing any such legitimacy to the FARC, and President Uribe has even gone so far as to deny that there is an armed conflict in Colombia. However, under the Protocol II amendment to the Geneva Conventions, international humanitarian law sidesteps the issue of recognition of belligerency by a government and considers all parties engaged in an internal armed conflict beholden to the Geneva Conventions if an insurgency has met the requirements for belligerent status, which the FARC has done.[67]

But the FARC has not been viewed as belligerents by the international community. In fact, following the 9/11 attacks, the Bush administration took an even harder line towards the FARC as the rebels were portrayed as 'narco-terrorists', an approach that was made easier with the election of Uribe. Furthermore, the regional shift to the left that was initiated by Venezuela would make Colombia even more geopolitically important to the United States. Consequently, officials in Washington and Bogotá, as well as the mainstream media in both countries, began portraying Colombia as the democratic and capitalist alternative to Chávez's Venezuelan socialist revolution. Accordingly, US and Colombian officials, and the mainstream media, intensified their focus on the FARC's human rights violations, particularly kidnapping, in an effort to portray the rebel group as a terrorist organization and a threat to democracy.

CHAPTER 6

The FARC and Human Rights

RENEWED EFFORTS by the US and Colombian governments to demonize the FARC under the war on terror had the desired impact. While there is widespread consensus among people across the political spectrum in Colombia that the FARC was an ideologically motivated insurgency in its early years, many people now argue that the FARC has lost its ideological focus and has simply become a criminal organization with no political objectives. Even many of those charged with combating the guerrillas, such as military officers and paramilitary leaders, claim that the FARC used to be ideologically motivated, as though such a view bolsters their argument that the guerrillas are now nothing more than criminals.[1] Ironically, many of these same people also accuse the FARC of being a terrorist group even though virtually every definition of terrorism requires that an act of violence be politically motivated in order to be considered an act of terrorism. There is no doubt that the FARC utilizes terrorist tactics and, as a result, perpetrates egregious human rights violations against the civilian population – as do all the actors in Colombia's armed conflict. But to what degree is perpetrating human rights abuses inevitable in an armed struggle? And what is the nature of those abuses?

In much the same way that the labels 'terrorist' or 'narco-terrorist' have been used as propaganda weapons, so have accusations of human rights abuses attributed to the FARC. The question, however, is not whether or not the FARC violates human rights – of that there is no doubt – but relates to the quantitative aspect of the human rights abuses and the distorted perceptions created by Colombian and US government officials and the mainstream media.

During the 1970s, the growing international spotlight on human rights, spurred in part by the horrendous abuses perpetrated by the Pinochet dictatorship in Chile, raised consciousness of the issue in both Colombia and the United States. By the following decade, international organizations such as Amnesty International and Human Rights Watch (known as Americas Watch at the time) successfully placed human rights on the US foreign policy agenda by linking US military aid to human rights violations perpetrated by the recipients of that aid. Up until that point in Colombia, the military had perpetrated most of the country's human rights violations without fear of political repercussions.

During the 1980s, in response to increasing concern among sectors of the US Congress over the disbursement of US military aid to Latin American militaries responsible for gross violations of human rights, the Colombian military sought to outsource its 'dirty war' to right-wing paramilitary death squads. This strategy was an attempt to present a 'clean' force suitable for receiving US military aid, while retaining the extrajudicial powers of a para-military force still engaged in a 'dirty' war. By the late 1980s, the paramilitaries had become the principal perpetrators of human rights abuses that included the murder of members of the political opposition, peasants and union leaders. But the FARC's actions also showed up on the human rights radar, primarily through its increasing involvement in kidnapping.

Human rights abuses in Colombia reached horrendous levels during the 1990s and the country became one of the most violent in the world. Massacres of civilians – the killing of four or more people in the same place at the same time – increased dramatically during the decade, peaking in 1999 when 403 occurred with 1,836 people killed.[2] According to the Colombian government's Ombudsman's Office, the paramilitaries were responsible for more than double the number of massacres attributed to both the FARC and the ELN.[3] Meanwhile, Human Rights Watch, utilizing statistics compiled by the Bogotá-based Colombian Commission of Jurists (CCJ), attributed 78 per cent of the human rights abuses and violations of international law in 1999 to the paramilitaries, with the guerrillas responsible for 20 per cent and state security forces for the remaining 2 per cent.[4]

Even the US State Department acknowledged the escalating levels of human rights abuses being perpetrated by the paramilitaries in its annual human rights report for 1999:

> Throughout the country, paramilitary groups killed, tortured, and threatened civilians suspected of sympathizing with guerrillas in an orchestrated campaign to terrorize them into fleeing their homes, thereby depriving guerrillas of civilian support. Paramilitary forces were responsible for an increasing number of massacres and other politically motivated killings.[5]

The State Department's report also acknowledged the collusion between the Colombian military and the paramilitaries, noting,

> At times the security forces collaborated with paramilitary groups that committed abuses; in some instances, individual members of the security forces actively collaborated with members of paramilitary groups by passing them through roadblocks, sharing intelligence,

and providing them with ammunition. Paramilitary forces find a ready support base within the military and police, as well as local civilian elites in many areas.[6]

Recently declassified documents make evident the degree to which the United States was aware of the Colombian military's collaboration with paramilitaries. In 1999, US ambassador Curtiss Kamman dispatched a cable to the State Department describing massacres in La Gabarra and Tibú that left as many as fifty people dead. The ambassador noted that '46th Battalion soldiers had donned AUC armbands the night of May 29 and participated directly in the La Gabarra massacre.'[7] In a February 1999 classified Defence Department document, a US military official acknowledged, 'The Colombian Armed Forces have not actively persecuted paramilitary group members because they see them as allies in the fight against the guerrillas, their common enemy.'[8] And in September of the same year, the CIA's Senior Executive Intelligence Brief echoed the Defence Department report, stating that local military commanders 'do not challenge paramilitary groups operating in their areas because they see the insurgents as the common foe'.[9]

In September 2001, Human Rights Watch published a report documenting the ties between the Colombian army's 24th Brigade in Putumayo and the paramilitaries. In the report, a former bookkeeper for the AUC detailed how payments were made to soldiers in the 24th Brigade based on rank: 'Each captain received between $2,000 and $3,000 per month. Majors got $2,500. A lieutenant receives $1,500. The colonels also got paid, but not directly. They would send intermediaries to pick up the cash.'[10] The bookkeeper claimed that the AUC's budget in Putumayo amounted to $650,000 a month and that most of the revenues were generated from cocaine processing labs located in areas under paramilitary control.[11]

Despite overwhelming evidence from Colombian and inter-national human rights organizations, and the US government's own internal documents, regarding the Colombian military's collusion with paramilitary death squads, US military aid to Co-lombia under the guise of the war on drugs continued unabated. In fact, it was in the midst of the violence being perpetrated by AUC paramilitaries allied with the US-backed Colombian military that Plan Colombia was devised as a response to the growing threat posed by the FARC.

In an effort to intensify the implementation of neoliberalism that was occurring under Plan Colombia and the war on terror, the US and Colombian governments signed a free-trade agreement in November 2006. However, ratification of the agreement by the US Congress stalled due to human rights concerns related to paramilitary violence. In essence, the agreement has become a symbolic battleground in which free-trade agreements are viewed as a prize awarded for human rights performance. Many Democrats in Congress and unions in the United States have opposed the agreement due to the fact that more labour leaders are killed annually in Colombia than in the rest of the world. However, the number of Colombian labour leaders killed each year has diminished significantly over the past decade. As US State Department spokesperson R. Nicholas Burns argued in October 2007, 'Homicides of trade unionists have shown a steep decline.... Rather than condemning as insufficient the consider-able progress already made by the Colombian people, we should help them consolidate that progress through expanded trade.'[12]

But the dirty war being waged against Colombia's union leaders, in conjunction with the implementation of neoliberal economic reforms, has devastated union organizations and their memberships. More than 195 trade-union organizations were dis-solved between 1991 and 2001, with union membership declining by more than 100,000 workers during that period. In fact, with only 4 per cent of the workforce unionized – compared to 15 per cent twenty years ago – Colombia now has the lowest unionization rate in Latin America.[13] In other words, more than twenty years of a dirty war waged against Colombia's unions by right-wing paramilitaries allied with the Colombian military has meant that there are fewer labour leaders left to kill. Consequently, opponents of the free-trade agreement do not believe that the Colombian government should be rewarded for the slaughter of the country's workers and that the rate of killings, while diminished, remains unacceptably high with Colombia accounting for 49 of the 76 labour leaders assassinated globally in 2008.[14]

Targeting Civilians

The paramilitaries have been responsible not only for most of the assassinations of labour leaders, but also for the majority of all human rights abuses perpetrated by irregular armed groups against the civilian population. However, the FARC is to blame for some of the violations. The principal human rights violation perpetrated by the FARC has been kidnapping, primarily of middle- and upper-class Colombians. The number of people kidnapped in Colombia peaked at the turn of the century and has declined dramatically in recent years. In 1999, for example, almost 3,000 people were kidnapped, with 728 cases attributed to the FARC, according to the Colombian NGO Free Country Foundation (Fundación País Libre).[15] But in 2007, the total number of kidnappings had fallen to 521 cases.[16]

An increase in human rights violations committed by the FARC at the end of the 1990s coincided with a dramatic rise in kidnappings perpetrated by the guerrilla group and the handing over of the safe haven to the rebels by the government of President

Pastrana.[17] Interestingly, there was a significant decline in the number of kidnappings perpetrated by the FARC in 2003, the year following the Pastrana government's termination of the peace process and the safe haven. While this reduction in kidnappings by the FARC has largely been attributed to the security policies of the Uribe administration, the timing of both the increase and the decline suggests that the guerrilla group's loss of a safe haven in which to safely stash hostages appears to have also been a significant contributing factor.

The FARC is not unique in its use of kidnapping as a political strategy. Both the Sandinista guerrillas in Nicaragua during the 1970s and the Farabundo Martí National Liberation Front (FMLN) in El Salvador the following decade, among others, kidnapped members of the political elite to use as bargaining chips in negotiations. Essentially, there are three categories of prisoners held by the FARC: high-profile political prisoners such as Ingrid Betancourt and other politicians and government officials; police and soldiers captured in battle whom the guerrillas consider to be prisoners of war; and kidnapped civilians who are held for ransoms, or 'war taxes', used to fund the insurgency. Those captives in the first two categories are political prisoners to be used as bargaining chips in negotiations with the government, while those in the third category are simply seized in order to generate revenue.

The FARC's strategy of using its political prisoners and captured enemy fighters as pawns at the negotiating table has been a failure. In fact, there has only been one prisoner exchange between the FARC and the government in the rebel group's more than four decades of existence. In 2001, the FARC released more than 242 police and soldiers in return for the liberation of 15 sick guerrillas. It is difficult for the FARC to argue that the political and tactical gains that resulted from this prisoner exchange offset the public backlash the rebel group has endured in response to its practice of holding kidnapped political figures and captured government troops in jungle camps for years. While the human rights violations related to holding civilians hostage are obvious, the issue of prisoners of war is not so clear. Captured police and soldiers are armed combatants in a civil conflict and their imprisonment by the FARC is not, in and of itself, a human rights violation. Of course, the conditions in which they are detained might well violate human rights norms under the Geneva Conventions.

Given the fact that there has been only one prisoner exchange agreement between the FARC and the government in more than forty years of conflict, it is questionable whether holding prisoners of war for years makes sense from either a public relations or a tactical perspective. After all, the practice not only results in a lot of bad publicity for the rebels, it also requires hundreds of guerrillas to guard the prisoners, thereby reducing the number of rebels available for military operations. The FARC might be wise to utilize Fidel Castro's strategy of simply disarming and releasing all police officers and soldiers captured in battle. This would not only be a public relations coup for the FARC, it would also contribute to undermining the morale of the Colombian armed forces. After all, there is little incentive to fight to the death if surrendering will result in one's immediate liberation rather than years of confinement in a jungle prison camp. This was a psychological strategy that Castro utilized to great advantage in the Sierra Maestra.

In addition to those politicians that it kidnaps for political purposes and the prisoners of war that it holds captive, the FARC has also abducted civilians to hold for ransom in order to help fund its insurgency. Those kidnapped to raise revenues are primarily from the middle and upper classes, since they are the ones best situated to pay ransoms and, from the class-conflict perspective of the FARC, constitute the sectors of the population that benefit from the country's gross social and economic inequalities. Unlike political kidnapping, this revenue-raising strategy has proven successful from a tactical perspective. However, it could be argued that the negative political and public image that has resulted from this strategy significantly outweighs the financial benefits accrued through the practice.

What is particularly troublesome for the FARC is the fact that it is not only the middle and upper classes that view the rebel group negatively with regard to the issue of kidnapping. Because kidnapping receives a disproportionate amount of media coverage – precisely because it is the wealthy rather than the poor who are the principal victims – most Colombians, including the poor, have come to view the practice as nothing more than a gross violation of human rights rather than as class warfare. As mentioned previously, the FARC's involvement in the kidnapping of civilians has diminished greatly in recent years, although it is not clear whether this represents a shift in guerrilla strategy or is due simply to the security climate no longer being as amenable to the practice of kidnapping. Ultimately, while the FARC justifies the kidnapping of middle- and upper-class civilians as a form of class warfare, the practice constitutes an act of violence against non-combatants and, in the eyes of many human rights groups, violates international humanitarian law.

The FARC, although on a smaller scale than the paramilitaries, has also been responsible for the killing of civilians through massacres and targeted assassinations. One high-profile human rights violation perpetrated by the FARC in 1999 was the killing of three US citizens who were helping the indigenous U'wa in northern Colombia in their struggle to prevent a US oil company from operating on their traditional lands. In February 1999, FARC guerrillas seized the three activists – Terry Freitas,

Ingrid Washinawatok and Lahe'ena'e Gay – and a week later transported them across the border into Venezuela and executed them. At first the FARC denied any involvement in the killings, but later confessed to the crime after the Colombian military released a tape of an intercepted radio conversation between a FARC commander and a subordinate in which the former ordered the killing of the three Americans.

Not surprisingly, the FARC refused to turn over the guerrillas involved in the killings to Colombian or US authorities, claiming that those responsible would be tried by a revolutionary tribunal. There is, however, no evidence that the commander who ordered the killings was held accountable for his actions. Such killings raise serious questions regarding the attitude of the FARC's Secretariat towards the actions of lower-level commanders. Are mid-level commanders making these decisions with the approval of the Secretariat? Or are mid-level commanders making these decisions unilaterally and in contradiction of the FARC's rules and regulations? And if this is the case, does the Secretariat hold them accountable after the fact? It is difficult to gain reliable insights into such inner workings of the FARC. However, in the case of the US human rights activists, the mid-level commander who ordered the killings, German Briceño, was the brother of Secretariat member Jorge Briceño, also known as Mono Jojoy, and in this instance it appears that the author of the crime was never brought before a revolutionary tribunal. It is unclear to what degree Mono Jojoy intervened on his brother's behalf, but it appears likely that he did. In many ways, Mono Jojoy epitomizes the contradiction that is the FARC. He is often portrayed in the media as the most ruthless and corrupt of the guerrilla group's Secretariat. At the same time, many of the FARC's most progressive social projects have been implemented in regions of eastern Colombia under his command.

Like the paramilitaries, the FARC often justifies its killing of civilians by accusing them of working with the enemy. While there is clearly a space for peasants and other residents living in regions traditionally controlled by the FARC to voice opinions that contradict the policies of the guerrilla group, the rebels have exhibited little or no tolerance for anyone they believe is colluding with the military or paramilitaries. In one such instance in June 2004, the FARC admitted to killing thirty-four coca farmers in the department of Norte de Santander. The farmers were tied up with ropes and then executed with automatic weapons. In a public statement, the FARC claimed the peasants were working with the paramilitaries. According to a government official, paramilitaries owned the farm where the massacre occurred, but it was unclear whether the peasants were simply earning a living or actively collaborating with the right-wing militia.[18]

Another example of the FARC's attitude towards those suspected of collaborating with the enemy was its massacre of indigenous Awa in the southern department of Nariño in February 2009. The FARC confessed to killing eight people, while the National Indigenous Organization of Colombia (Organización Nacional Indígena de Colombia, ONIC) claimed twenty-seven were massacred. In a statement, the FARC said it executed the eight indigenous because their collaboration with the Colombian military had led to the deaths of several guerrillas. The ONIC responded by stating that Colombian soldiers operating in the region had forced members of the community to reveal information about the location of the guerrillas and that they were innocent neutrals caught in the middle of the conflict.[19]

Most of those killed in Colombia's armed conflict have been unarmed civilians that one side or the other claimed were sympathetic to, or working with, the enemy. Many human rights organizations paint a black-and-white picture of Colombia's dirty war by earnestly portraying the indigenous, NGO workers, unionists and other members of civil society as neutral with regard to the armed conflict involving the guerrillas, the military and the paramilitaries. In reality, the situation is much more complex. While many indigenous and civil society members are adamantly opposed to armed struggle and are innocent victims of government, paramilitary and guerrilla violence, there are some who are sympathetic towards, and even collaborate with, the armed actors.

On the one hand, many among Colombia's political and military elite view everyone engaged non-violently in the struggle for social justice as guerrillas and use this rationale to justify waging a dirty war. On the other hand, many human rights groups and NGO organizations claim that almost all members of civil society are struggling non-violently for change and are not affiliated with any of the armed groups. The reality lies somewhere between these two positions; exactly where is not clear because of the necessity for anyone sympathetic to the guerrillas to act clandestinely. Nevertheless, one thing is absolutely clear under international law: the killing of an unarmed person, even an active participant in the conflict, by any armed actor constitutes a violation of international humanitarian law. And the FARC has often perpetrated such violations against the very class of Colombians that it claims, as the 'People's Army', to represent.

Another controversial human rights issue related to the FARC has been the rebel group's recruitment of child soldiers. Human rights organizations consider any soldier under the age of 18 to be a child combatant based on the Optional Protocol to the UN Convention on the Rights of the Child, to which Colombia is a signatory. The FARC, however, does not recognize the Optional Protocol, and claims to abide by Article 38 of the Convention, which prohibits the recruitment of anyone under the age of 15.[20]

In 2003, Human Rights Watch estimated that there were more than 11,000 child combatants under 18 belonging to guerrilla and paramilitary groups in Colombia.[21] The FARC is believed to have the largest number of child combatants in its ranks, partly because it is the largest armed group. According to Human Rights Watch, 'Internal FARC–EP regulations stipulate that 15 is the minimum age for recruitment, which is in line with the norms of international humanitarian law. Yet the guerrillas have never respected the minimum age requirement, despite repeated promises to do so.'[22]

Nancy Springer, a law professor at Jorge Tadeo Lozano University in Bogotá, has interviewed more than eight thousand guerrillas who were captured or deserted since 2002. She concurs with Human Rights Watch's conclusions, claiming that 43 per cent of the FARC members she interviewed joined the guerrilla group when they were 14 or younger and a disproportionate percentage were indigenous youths.[23] One former indigenous child combatant from the highlands of the department of Cauca explained that he joined the FARC because 'they're always around and they have a better image than the army, which only comes up here to harass people'.[24] But once in the ranks of the guerrillas, child combatants in the FARC have the same responsibilities as adult fighters. A former FARC guerrilla named Julian, who joined when he was 16, said, 'Life with the rebels is hard. You don't sleep, you're always hungry, and if you make a mistake they bring you before a war council. The penalties can be doing extra guard duty or going before a firing squad.'[25]

FARC commander Simón Trinidad insists that the guerrilla group does not intentionally recruit anybody under 15 years of age, although he concedes that it likely occurs because many children who enlist do not have identification to prove their age. In defence of the FARC's regulations that permit the recruitment of children between 15 and 18 years of age, Trinidad argues, 'It sounds beautiful when you say that children shouldn't be guerrillas, but the children are in the streets of the cities doing drugs, inhaling gasoline and glue. They are highly exploited.... In the guerrillas we have dignity, respect and we provide them with clothes, food and education.'[26] A Human Rights Watch report on child combatants in Colombia reflects the justifications offered by Trinidad for recruiting minors:

> Irregular forces exploit children's vulnerability.... Some families send children to combat because they are unable to support them, and they know that membership in an armed group guarantees a square meal, clothing, and protection. Many children join to escape family violence and physical or sexual abuse, or to find the affection their families fail to give.[27]

There has been a great deal of propaganda put out by Colombian government and military officials, and also by the mainstream media, accusing the FARC of forcibly recruiting children into its ranks. But FARC commander Raúl Reyes denies that the guerrilla group forcibly recruits children, arguing that it would undermine its fighting capacity and even place commanders at risk. According to Reyes,

> The FARC never forces anybody to join; it is completely contrary to our safety regulations. Why would I give a weapon to someone that has been forced to join and then tell him he has to be my bodyguard? The guard is going to make me pay right there with that weapon. It never happens. This is disinformation from these organizations. What happens to cause this disinformation? In many cases there are boys and girls that join and then later, for one reason or another, they decide to leave. Life here is very hard, one must be disciplined. Perhaps they had family that they couldn't see, a son or a daughter, or a boyfriend, or a girlfriend. Or they thought that this struggle would be easy and then they aren't willing to sacrifice, so they leave.... then, in many cases, they

are going to say that they were forced to join in order to defend themselves against the repression of the police and also, in many cases, of their families.[28]

Every major report on the issue of child combatants in Colombia has concluded, as did Human Rights Watch, that 'the great majority of child recruits to the irregular forces decide to join voluntarily', although 'the voluntary decision to join irregular forces is more a reflection of the dismal lack of opportunities open to children from the poorest sector of rural society than a real exercise of free will'.[29]

Researcher Ingunn Bjørkhaug also concludes that the majority of children that join Colombia's armed groups enlist voluntarily. However, engaging in a slightly more nuanced examination of child recruitment in Colombia's armed conflict, she argues that 'most cases of recruitment take place in the grey zone between voluntary and coerced recruitment', in what she has labelled as 'voluntarily forced'.[30] Bjørkhaug argues that children are not coerced in the conventional sense of the term, rather that they make their choices based on their particular experiences and circumstances.

The contexts that could lead a child to enlist in an armed group range from the desire to escape abuse, poverty and other socio-economic misfortunes, to being manipulated by the armed groups. In some cases, children living in regions controlled by the FARC would be expected to attend meetings and receive some basic training. They might also be integrated into the guerrilla group's militia units before becoming full-time, uniformed fighters. FARC militia members live ostensibly civilian lives in villages and cities where they often act as the eyes and ears of the guerrilla group and help organize logistics related to the delivery of food, ammunition and other essential supplies to full-time units. According to Bjørkhaug:

The pressure on the families would vary from village to village, depending on the stronghold of the group. In particular, FARC used this method to recruit children and allowed them to live at home during the training period. This period could last up to two years, and then the children were permanently moved into the armed group. The children were voluntarily forced as they felt obliged to join and feared the consequences of rejection. However, the child soldiers who grew up under such circumstances had a sense of fighting for a cause.[31]

While the overwhelming majority of children enlist in the FARC voluntarily – and there are many cases in which the child is younger than 15 – aggressive recruitment methods, abuse at home and poor socio-economic conditions may easily lead a child to believe that there are no viable alternatives. Furthermore, life in the guerrillas can even seem adventurous and romantic to an adolescent. As a Human Rights Watch report acknowledges, 'Camp life promises adventure, comradeship, and a chance to prove oneself.' Yet, as it also points out, 'The reality of life as a combatant is deeply frightening. But once incorporated, children cannot leave voluntarily. To the contrary, they know that the price of attempting to desert could be their lives.'[32]

Civilians as 'collateral damage'

The term 'collateral damage' was coined by the US military and has been applied since World War II to civilians unintentionally killed by military operations. In many cases, a military operation is aimed at a legitimate military target but unintentionally kills or wounds civilians in the process. The Protocol I amendment of the Geneva Conventions requires that parties engaged in an international conflict take due diligence with regard to the potential for causing civilian casualties; in other words, they must ensure that the collateral damage is in proportion to the military advantage gained by the operation. However, this vague and subjective requirement under Protocol I applies only to international conflicts and not to internal armed conflicts.[33]

Many of the civilians killed in military operations conducted by the FARC are 'collateral damage' resulting from the guerrilla group's use of landmines and home-made mortars. Since 2006, Colombia has been the world's leader in annual landmine casualties and it is estimated that there are more than 100,000 anti-personnel landmines in the country. There were 6,696 reported landmine casualties between 1999 and 2008, with military personnel accounting for 70 per cent of them, although the total number of victims has been decreasing since 2006.[34] The Colombian government is a signatory to the Mine Ban Treaty and, in order to meet its obligations, has ceased production and is slowly dismantling the minefields surrounding military bases. The FARC, however, does not recognize the legitimacy of the Treaty and is the principal user of landmines in Colombia, followed by the ELN and the paramilitaries. In fact, according to the Landmine and Cluster Munition Monitor, 'FARC is probably the most prolific current user of antipersonnel mines among rebel groups anywhere in the world'.[35]

The FARC uses home-made landmines manufactured from easily obtainable materials. Many of the landmines are pressure-activated mines that are either chemically or electronically detonated. A canister, often an empty food can, is filled with shrapnel and an explosive compound, usually Indugel Plus. A plastic syringe is inserted into the top of the can, which is then buried in the ground with only the top of the syringe's plunger left exposed. When a victim steps on the syringe, sulphuric acid is injected into the detonator if it is a chemical device, or a connection is made to a small battery if it is electronic, and the mine explodes. The mines are known as *quiebrapatas*, or leg-breakers, because most victims lose a leg, although one in four loses their life. Human rights groups are opposed to the use of landmines because they kill indiscriminately, unable to determine the difference between a combatant and non-combatant.

Given the fact that peasants are dependent on their physical abilities to engage in farming, the loss of a leg can prove devastating, not only economically but also psychologically. Consequently, landmine victims and their families often abandon their farms because of fear and an inability to work the land due to their physical disability. The newly displaced families find themselves in unfamiliar urban environments where their lack of education and job skills leaves them in a desperate struggle to survive as they are forced to work in the informal economy.

When representatives from the NGO Colombia's Campaign Against Landmines (Campaña Colombiana Contra Minas, CCCM) raised the issue of landmines with the FARC, the rebels claimed that mines are weapons of the poor, and said that when the government stops using bombs, planes and satellites, then they will stop using mines.[36] The FARC is unlikely to stop using landmines in the near future because it is by far the most effective weapon in the guerrilla group's arsenal. Under President Uribe, the Colombian military became more aggressive in its counter-insurgency operations and the FARC has increasingly turned to landmines as a means of slowing military offensives. As a result, the number of Colombian soldiers killed by landmines has risen steadily, increasing by 15 per cent between 2008 and 2009. But while landmines might be an effective weapon for the FARC, and a majority of the victims are combatants, a significant number of civilians are maimed and killed each year by them.

Human rights groups have also criticized the FARC for its use of home-made mortars. These mortars are known as *cilindros*, or cylinder bombs, because they are made from the long cylindrical metal gas canisters that are commonly used to supply homes with cooking fuel in rural Colombia. The guerrilla group has frequently used its home-made cylinder bombs to attack police stations in rural towns and villages. The principal problem with the weapon is that it is notoriously inaccurate and frequently misses its intended target, often killing civilians in adjacent buildings. Despite this reality, the FARC has continued to utilize cylinder bombs, arguing that they are being used to attack legitimate military targets.

In essence the FARC views civilian casualties in much the same way that the US military views non-combatants killed by its air strikes in Iraq and Afghanistan: as unfortunate collateral damage. According to FARC commander Reyes,

> The FARC does not have heavy armaments; the FARC, as you know, has still not been recognized as a belligerent force and cannot obtain the armaments that it should possess as an army. So it develops a lot of home-made armaments to use against the public forces.... Many times those who operate these apparatuses, the cylinder bombs or other weapons, commit errors. They aim at the police station but they strike the neighbouring house.... It's lamentable, of course. There is not a single justification for it. But they are human failings, caused by the nervousness of whoever is launching it or a failure in the structure of the cylinder bomb. This is a failure that has occurred and we are trying to correct it so that these mistakes that affect the population won't happen.[37]

Human rights groups, however, have called on the FARC to stop using home-made cylinder bombs because their inaccuracy makes them indiscriminate killers that cannot differentiate between military objectives and non-combatants. José Miguel Vivanco, director of the Americas programme at Human Rights Watch, stated: 'The FARC–EP's continued use of gas cylinder bombs shows this armed group's flagrant disregard for lives of civilians. The FARC must immediately cease these horrific attacks, which violate the most basic principles of the laws of war.'[38]

One of the most infamous and tragic incidents related to the FARC's use of cylinder bombs occurred in May 2002 in the village of Bellavista in the western department of Chocó. Bellavista is situated in the municipality of Boyaja deep in the jungle on the Atrato river, which is the region's principal transportation artery. The problem began when 400 AUC paramilitaries made their way up the river to Bellavista and neighbouring Vigia del Fuerte in late April. They passed unhindered through an army checkpoint in Ríosucio, just a few hours downriver from their destination in guerrilla-controlled territory. Bellavista's acting mayor, Manuel Corrales, described the arrival of the paramilitaries on 21 April 2002: 'They said they weren't there to attack us; that they weren't going to kill anyone like before when they chopped off heads and cut open torsos. That they were here to confront the guerrillas and to get them out of the community.'[39] Knowing the local population would inevitably be caught in the middle of a battle between the guerrillas and the paramilitaries, Corrales notified regional and national authorities of the impending danger to the community, but 'the government, the state and the public forces didn't do anything'.[40]

Fighting began ten days later on 1 May when FARC guerrillas attempted to drive the paramilitaries out of Bellavista and Vigia del Fuerte in an offensive that lasted throughout the night and into the next day. In an attempt to avoid getting caught in the crossfire, hundreds of Bellavista residents fled from a northern barrio to seek refuge in a church in the town centre. On the second day, the FARC launched a cylinder bomb at a group of paramilitaries that had set up camp next to the church, but the projectile missed its target and crashed through the roof of the adjacent building. In consequence 119 people were killed, almost 10 per cent of the town's population.

Government troops did not arrive in Bellavista until six days after the fighting had ended, despite the fact that the 12th Infantry Battalion belonging to the Colombian army's Fourth Brigade was based in Quibdó, only four hours upriver by motorboat. Furthermore, paramilitaries remained in the town for two weeks after the army arrived. A report issued by the UN human rights envoy to Colombia, Anders Kompass, who visited Bellavista a week after the attack, criticized the government's failure to respond to the paramilitary presence in the town.[41] Corrales corroborated the UN report, claiming that after the church bombing the 'paramilitaries remained here for about twenty days. Then some paramilitary boats showed up and took them all away, including the injured.'[42]

While Corrales was critical of the army's lack of response to the paramilitary incursion, the town's acting mayor held the FARC primarily responsible for the tragedy: 'It's clear that those cylinder bombs are not accurate. They knew that they were putting the population in danger. The people are convinced that they knew those people were in the church.'[43] The UN also blamed the FARC, accusing the guerrilla group of perpetrating a war crime for targeting a part of town heavily populated with civilians. As author Mario Murillo pointed out, 'Although the FARC acknowledged it as an "accident," the bombing points to the destructive nature of their reckless use of these types of rudimentary weapons in civilian areas.'[44]

Meanwhile, the Colombian government has sought to utilize the Bellavista tragedy for propaganda purposes. The army erected a massive sign on the bank of the river in Bellavista stating: 'On 2 May 2002, the FARC assassinated 119 people here. We will never forget.' Clearly, by using the word 'assassinated' instead of 'killed', the army is attempting to create the impression that the FARC intentionally targeted the victims. Four days after the attack, Colombia's President Pastrana declared: 'This was a massacre, a genocide by the FARC, that attacked a civilian population that had taken refuge in a church.'[45] The Colombian army later published a report entitled 'Bojaya: FARC Genocide'. According to human rights expert Winifred Tate,

> 'Boyaja: FARC Genocide' is one example of the frequent misuse of the legal terminology of international human rights norms by the Colombian military in an apparent effort to make its claims more dramatic. Combat in which soldiers are killed is called a massacre; guerrilla attacks against government offices in small towns, which often kill numerous civilians because of the use of inaccurate weapons such as home-made cylinder bombs and car bombs, is called genocide.[46]

Distorted Perceptions of Human Rights Abuses

In an armed conflict such as the one in Colombia, propaganda is an important weapon. It is difficult for journalists and analysts to investigate independently the reality on the ground and so statistics and information are obtained from a variety of sources in order to draw conclusions. However, the mainstream media in the United States is often overreliant on two sources: Colombian and US government officials. Not surprisingly, then, it is the perspectives of the Colombian and US governments that dominate most news reports. By comparing human rights reports with media coverage of Colombia's violence, it is possible to understand why and how the public's perception of the conflict has been distorted.

The Bogotá-based Centre for Research and Popular Education (Centro de Investigación y Educación Popular, CINEP), a leading Jesuit-run think-tank that monitors Colombia's conflict and political violence, has documented the number of violations of international humanitarian law (killings of civilians, forced displacements, disappearances, kidnappings, arbitrary arrests, etc.) perpetrated by each armed actor between 1990 and 2007. Throughout the 1990s, the paramilitaries were by far the leading violator of international humanitarian law, accounting for 53 per cent of the 6,059 documented violations between 1990 and 1998 that were attributed to them, the military or the FARC. During the same period, the FARC was responsible for 27 per cent and the military for 20 per cent – although, because the military regularly colluded with the paramilitaries, the total share of violations perpetrated in defence of the state is 73 per cent.[47]

During the ensuing four years, the number of violations by all three armed actors increased, with the paramilitaries and the FARC showing the greatest proliferation. The increase in violations committed by the FARC during this period consisted of a dramatic rise in kidnappings that, as previously noted, coincided with the handing over of the safe haven to the rebels by the government of President Pastrana.[48] In 2003, the year following the Pastrana government's termination of the peace process and the safe haven, there was a significant decline in the number of kidnappings perpetrated by the FARC. According to CINEP, overall human rights violations perpetrated by the FARC declined from 40 per cent of the national total in 2002 – before the drop in kidnappings – to only 10 per cent in 2006. These numbers suggest that kidnapping has constituted the principal human rights abuse perpetrated by the guerrillas and its reduction meant that the FARC was responsible for fewer violations of international humanitarian law in 2006 than in any year since 1990.

President Uribe's first four-year term in office (2002–06) also saw a significant decrease in human rights abuses perpetrated by paramilitaries, most likely as a result of the demobilization process that the government initiated with the AUC in 2003. But while the total number of human rights violations perpetrated by the paramilitaries declined between 2002 and 2006, the percentage of abuses that the right-wing death squads were responsible for remained fairly constant – 31 per cent in 2002 and 29 per cent four years later – even though they were supposedly engaged in a ceasefire and a demobilization.[49]

The Colombian government claims that the paramilitaries have now demobilized, but according to many analysts the disbandment of the AUC represented little more than a restructuring of the death squads. The Colombian NGO Indepaz, for instance, reported in 2006 that 43 new paramilitary groups totalling almost 4,000 fighters had formed in 23 of the country's 32 departments.[50] Meanwhile, the following year, the Organization of American States (OAS) estimated that there were 20 new paramilitary groups with 3,000 fighters operating in Colombia.[51]

While the Uribe administration dismisses these new armed groups as criminal organizations and not as actors engaged in an armed conflict, one of Colombia's leading human rights lawyers, Alirio Uribe, of the José Alvear Restrepo Lawyers' Collective, disagrees:

> There are forty-three new paramilitary groups but, according to the Ministry of Defence, these new paramilitary groups have nothing to do with the old ones. But the truth is, they are the same. Before they were the AUC, now they are called the New Generation AUC. They have the same collusion with the army and the police. It's a farce.[52]

Perhaps the most startling statistic with regard to violations of international humanitarian law is the dramatic escalation in the direct role played in abuses by the Colombian state in recent years. According to CINEP, the state was responsible for 17 per cent of all violations when President Uribe assumed office in

2002. Four years later, at the end of Uribe's first term, it was responsible for 56 per cent of abuses – almost double the number of total violations perpetrated by state agents in 2002. Meanwhile, the paramilitaries and the FARC accounted for 29 per cent and 10 per cent respectively.[53]

These statistics often stand in stark contrast to the picture presented in the media, where an endless stream of quotations by Colombian and US officials repeatedly refer to the 'brutality' of the FARC 'terrorists' while rarely ever mentioning abuses perpetrated by the military and the paramilitaries. For instance, whenever killings of civilians occur, Colombian officials immediately blame the FARC. The mainstream media then dutifully report the accusations without initiating their own investigation of the crimes. And in those cases in which evidence finally emerges showing that it was actually the Colombian military or the paramilitaries that committed the killings, the lack of government focus on the new revelations usually results in the mainstream media failing to report the revised findings, thereby leaving in place the impression that the FARC was the guilty party.

This propaganda strategy utilized by the Colombian government – with the acquiescence of the mainstream media – has led to people's perception of the conflict becoming disconnected from the human rights reality on the ground. People are overwhelmed with news stories about killings allegedly perpetrated by the guerrillas, while there are significantly fewer accounts of ongoing abuses by the Colombian military and its paramilitary allies.

A study of the killings of civilians clearly illustrates the chasm between the reality on the ground and the media's portrayal of the violence. During President Uribe's first term in office (2002–06), the *New York Times* published twenty-one news reports that specifically referred to the killing of civilians in Colombia. Seventeen of the reports held the guerrillas responsible for the killings referred to in the articles, while the paramilitaries were blamed in two cases, the military in one, and both the rebels and paramilitaries in the remaining instance. In every one of the seventeen articles in which the guerrillas were held responsible, the only sources cited were Colombian government or military officials.[54]

However, according to a 2007 report published by the Colombian Commission of Jurists (CCJ), the guerrillas were responsible for 25 per cent of the killings of civilians during President Uribe's first term in office. Meanwhile, the paramilitaries accounted for 61 per cent of the deaths and the Colombian military for the remaining 14 per cent.[55] These numbers differ dramatically from the picture presented by the *New York Times*, which created the impression that the guerrillas were responsible for 80 per cent rather than 25 per cent of the killings. Meanwhile, the *Times* articles implied that the paramilitaries were responsible for only 10 per cent of the murders and the military for a mere 5 per cent.

An overreliance on official sources and the resulting distorted portrayal of human rights violations is not unique to the *New York Times*; it is present in most mainstream US media coverage. Official press junkets, regularly organized by the Colombian military and the US embassy, are a convenient way for foreign correspondents based in Bogotá to visit remote rural regions affected by the armed conflict. The problem with this arrangement, however, is that the journalists are flown to a specific destination chosen by the authorities, where they spend a few hours with officials and get presented with a prepackaged story. Inevitably, the official line dominates the published account. For their part, the Colombian government and the US embassy are fully aware of the mainstream media's overreliance on official sources and so they regularly hold press conferences or dispatch officials to public events such as the launching of a new military operation.

Government officials realize that the media will obediently cover these events because they provide convenient stories for reporters working under tight deadlines.

The foreign correspondents based in Colombia often attend the same event or press junket in order to avoid being the only reporter not covering that particular 'story'. Consequently, several almost identical versions of the same article are published the following day by various US media outlets. Government officials know that if they keep the media occupied daily with prepackaged stories that portray government policy in a positive light, then reporters will be too busy to conduct deeper investigative journalism or focus their attention on those issues that officials would prefer to have ignored.

With the partial exception of the *Washington Post*'s Scott Wilson, who during his time in the country occasionally ventured out into rural conflict zones and presented alternative perspectives on the political situation, mainstream media correspondents in Colombia appear to view their journalistic responsibility in much the same way that *New York Times* reporter Judith Miller did in the lead-up to the war in Iraq. When asked why her articles often did not include the views of experts sceptical of the Bush administration's claims about weapons of mass destruction, Miller replied: 'My job isn't to assess the government's information and be an independent intelligence analyst myself. My job is to tell readers of the *New York Times* what the government thought of Iraq's arsenal.'[56] Unfortunately, in many cases, the media have displayed a similar lack of inquisitiveness about some of the larger factors at play in Colombia's armed conflict, often acting more like stenographers for government officials than journalists independently investigating stories.

The mainstream media not only exhibit bias towards the government's perspective; they also tend to reflect the views of

Colombia's dominant social and economic sectors. For example, the issue of kidnapping has received widespread media coverage because leftist guerrillas are the principal perpetrators among the armed groups and the victims are primarily politicians, members of the state security forces, and civilians from the urban middle and upper classes. While kidnapped Colombians are clearly victims of the country's violence and their plight deserves attention, their numbers pale in comparison to the number of peasants who have been forcibly displaced, mostly by the military and right-wing paramilitaries.

In 2000, at the outset of Plan Colombia, approximately three thousand Colombians were being kidnapped annually. Meanwhile, more than a quarter of a million peasants were being forcibly displaced from their homes and land every year, mostly by paramilitaries. And yet most people were oblivious to the fact that Colombia, with more than 3 million displaced people, had the second largest internally displaced population in the world – after Sudan.

And while the number of people kidnapped dropped to 521 in 2007, the number of Colombians being forcibly displaced was rising.[57] According to the Human Rights and Displacement Consultancy (Consultoría para los Derechos Humanos y Desplazamiento, CODHES), 305,966 people were forcibly displaced in 2007 – a startling 38 per cent increase over the previous year.[58] And yet, despite this reality, media coverage remained firmly focused on the plight of the kidnapped because the Uribe administration successfully kept the spotlight on the FARC's hostages and away from displaced Colombians, increasing numbers of whom have been forced from their homes by the Colombian military's aggressive counter-insurgency operations. Compared to their extensive coverage of kidnapping, the mainstream media have mostly ignored the plight of poor rural Colombians.

It is not only Colombian and US government officials and the media that have contributed to a distortion of the human rights reality in Colombia, but also international human rights organizations. Throughout the latter decades of the twentieth century, most human rights organizations saw their primary responsibility as holding the state accountable for human rights abuses in violation of international treaties to which it was a signatory. As human rights expert Winifred Tate has noted, many activists

> focused on the state-sponsored abuses as the one area of society they have leverage over as citizen-activists. In their view, only the state is party to human rights treaties; as the only body responsible for protecting human rights, only states should be held accountable for human rights violations.[59]

By the mid-1990s, however, an internal debate was occurring within human rights organizations regarding whether or not to focus also on human rights violations perpetrated by non-state actors such as the FARC and the ELN guerrillas in Colombia. Guerrilla kidnappings of foreigners had resulted in representatives from the international community – funders and government officials – placing pressure on Colombian NGOs to begin highlighting rebel abuses. At the time, Colombian NGOs were participating in bi-monthly meetings with foreign embassy officials, who were pressuring them to denounce guerrilla kidnappings. According to Tate, 'The stakes are high in these debates, in terms of both gaining domestic constituencies and gaining international support. Access to financial resources can be dependent on the adoption of a professional profile.'[60]

The shift from focusing on the violations of humanitarian law by the state and its paramilitary allies to emphasizing abuses by all the armed actors forced human rights workers to take a political stand. As Tate notes,

For activists, these debates also signal a shift in political identity and culture; they must decide whether or not they align themselves with radical left movements for social transformation or with an international movement that uses human rights norms to protect vulnerable citizens, establish accountability, and work for social transformation through the defense of the rule of law.[61]

By the late 1990s, it had become the norm for human rights groups and NGOs to focus on violations of international humanitarian law by all the armed actors in Colombia's conflict. Some of those activists in the human rights community who were opposed to using international humanitarian law to criticize the guerrillas believed that such a shift would make it easier for government officials to deflect attention away from the state's abuses and responsibilities and to focus it on the rebels. As previously noted, the Colombian and US governments have successfully distorted the portrayal of Colombia's human rights situation in the media. Perhaps just as troubling, however, is that the decision by activists to focus also on guerrilla abuses appears to have contributed to gross distortions of Colombia's human rights reality by international human rights organizations.

In the second paragraph of the Colombia section of its *World Report 2000*, Human Rights Watch stated:

> In 1999, paramilitaries were considered responsible for 78 per cent of the total number of human rights and international humanitarian law violations, according to the Colombian Commission of Jurists (Comisión Colombiana de Juristas, CCJ), a human rights group. For their part, guerrillas were credited with 20 per cent. State forces were linked to 2 per cent.[62]

In its report, Human Rights Watch provided quantitative data related to human rights violations in Colombia through its reference to CCJ. Furthermore, this data made evident that the paramilitaries were responsible for an overwhelming majority of the country's human rights abuses. But five years later, Human Rights Watch opened its report on Colombia by stating:

> Colombia's forty-year internal armed conflict continues to be accompanied by widespread violations of human rights and international humanitarian law. All actors in the conflict – guerrillas, paramilitary groups, and the armed forces – commit serious violations, such as massacres, assassinations, and kidnappings.[63]

In this report, Human Rights Watch lumped together all three armed actors – guerrillas, paramilitaries and the military – thereby suggesting that each was equally responsible for Colombia's human rights crisis. At no point in the remainder of the report was there any quantitative data assigning responsibility for the number of violations to each armed actor even though Colombian NGOs including CCJ and CINEP continued to make such information available. The following year, in its 2006 report, Human Rights Watch declared: 'Colombia's irregular armed groups, both guerrillas and paramilitaries, are responsible for the bulk of the human rights violations.'[64] Once again, Human Rights Watch failed to cite any reputable Colombian NGOs such as CCJ, which would later contradict Human Rights Watch by reporting that the state, not the guerrillas and paramilitaries, had become responsible for the majority of the human rights abuses by 2006.

And then, in the opening paragraph of the Colombia section of its *World Report 2009*, Human Rights Watch gave priority to the violations of international humanitarian law perpetrated by the guerrillas:

> Colombia's internal armed conflict continues to result in widespread abuses by irregular armed groups and government forces. The Colombian government dealt serious blows to the Revolutionary Armed Forces of Colombia (FARC) guerrillas in 2008. But guerrillas

continued to engage in kidnappings, use of antipersonnel landmines, recruitment of child combatants, and other abuses.[65]

In nine years, Human Rights Watch went from providing quantitative data holding the paramilitaries responsible for the overwhelming majority of Colombia's human rights violations to implying that the guerrillas were the primary perpetrators of abuses. This shift occurred during the same time frame that reports issued by reputable Colombian NGOs – the same ones that Human Rights Watch had previously cited – noted that the state had become the leading violator of international humanitarian law and that the percentage of abuses perpetrated against the civilian population by the guerrillas had diminished significantly.

Ultimately, in a conflict such as Colombia's, it is often impossible to define clearly who is a civilian and who is a military target. Paramilitary and guerrilla fighters often dress as civilians; non-combatants provide information and logistical support to the armed actors; legislators pass bills that authorize military repression; individuals and businesses provide funding to armed groups; and all of these actions contribute directly to violence against the civilian population. This reality led one Colombian human rights lawyer to ask, 'Who is outside of the conflict? How can we distinguish who is part of the war and who is not? In the logic of IHL [international humanitarian law], everything is untouchable.'[66]

The brutal reality of war is that civilians – particularly suspected collaborators – will inevitably be targeted. And while many human rights advocates seek to draw a neat line between the civilian population and armed actors, the boundary between the two is, in reality, often very murky. Therefore, the only realistic objective of international humanitarian law is to minimize to the greatest extent possible the degree to which unarmed people are targeted. In Colombia's case, the state has not only failed to meet its obligations to defend the human rights of its citizens, it has actually become the principal violator of those rights by repeatedly targeting members of civil society without providing sufficient evidence that they are actually linked to the guerrillas.

For its part, the FARC has violated international humanitarian law and there are often valid justifications for holding the guerrilla group accountable for its targeting of the civilian population. However, the degree to which it is responsible for abuses must also be contextualized. The failure of the media and international human rights organizations to contextualize effectively the number of violations perpetrated by the FARC has resulted in a gross distortion of Colombia's human rights reality. This has created the impression that, at best, all the armed actors are equally responsible or, at worst, that the guerrillas are the principal violators of international humanitarian law. In either case, this distortion has brought about the scenario that some activists warned against in the 1990s during the debate about whether or not human rights organizations should restrict their investigations to the actions of the state: it has aided government officials in their efforts to deflect attention away from the state's abuses and responsibilities and to focus it disproportionately on those violations perpetrated by the FARC.

CHAPTER 7

The Future of the FARC

On 1 March 2008, the Colombian military finally succeeded in killing a member of the FARC's Secretariat when it launched a cross-border airstrike into Ecuador that resulted in the death of the guerrilla group's number two commander Raúl Reyes. While the Colombian and US governments heralded the death of such a high-ranking FARC commander, others accused Colombia of violating international law by invading Ecuador's sovereignty. Six days after Reyes was killed, it was revealed that another member of the FARC's Secretariat, Iván Ríos, had died at the hands of his own security chief in the central Colombian department of Caldas. And then, on 26 March, the FARC's 80-year-old commander-in-chief Manuel Marulanda died of a heart attack in the jungles of eastern Colombia. It was the worst month in the FARC's long history, and for many analysts it signalled the beginning of the end for the guerrilla group.

Three months later, the Colombian military launched an audacious rescue operation that liberated fifteen high-profile captives held by the FARC, including former presidential candidate Ingrid Betancourt (who had been held for six years) and three US military contractors who had spent five years in jungle prison camps after their plane crashed in southern Colombia. The Colombian military had successfully infiltrated the FARC's internal communications network and convinced the commander of the rebel unit guarding the captives that the group's Secretariat had authorized the release of the prisoners to representatives of an international NGO. Once again, the government and its supporters cheered the success of the rescue mission, while some analysts criticized what appeared to be another violation of international law due to the misuse of the symbol of the International Committee of the Red Cross in the military operation.

The unprecedented hostage rescue seemed to confirm the predictions of many mainstream analysts that the FARC was crumbling. Following the rescue operation, Michael Shifter, vice president of the Washington DC-based Inter-American Dialogue, told *Time* magazine: 'This removes the only real bargaining chip the FARC had left in its dealings with the government. It's going to be very hard now to talk of the FARC as a national guerrilla movement – it's going to fracture and fragment even more.'[1]

The FARC's political chief Alfonso Cano replaced Marulanda as commander-in-chief and the other two vacancies in the Secretariat were quickly filled by experienced rebel commanders. But the military kept up the pressure on the battlefield and captured or killed several mid-level rebel commanders and, in September 2010, even succeeded in killing another member of the guerrilla group's Secretariat, Mono Jojoy.

There is no question that the guerrillas have been hurt by an increasingly aggressive Colombian military, which has benefited from more than $7 billion in US aid and training over the past decade. The FARC's influence in regions where it expanded its presence during the 1980s and 1990s has been either completely eliminated or has significantly diminished in recent years. The

FARC's focus on a military presence in most of these regions led to local populations viewing the guerrillas as outsiders. The failure to establish close social ties to the local populations allowed the newly strengthened Colombian military to defeat the FARC in those regions because the necessary civilian support for the rebels was lacking. As a result, the guerrilla's visible presence in northern and central Colombia as well as in the far eastern departments of Guainía, Vaupés and Amazonas has been virtually eradicated, although it is difficult to determine to what extent the FARC is operating clandestinely in these regions. The FARC's failure to move beyond a military presence in these regions was exemplified in the attitude of an indigenous leader in Guainía when he stated, 'The guerrillas never did anything for us.'[2]

By the end of 2010, the FARC maintained a significant presence in only three regions of the country: the south-east (Meta, Guaviare, Caquetá and Putumayo); the south-central highlands (Huila and southern Tolima); and the south-west (Nariño, Valle de Cauca and southern Chocó). Even in these traditional strongholds where the FARC remains organically linked to the peasant population, the guerrillas have been forced to retreat to the most remote regions. Nevertheless, the FARC's military strength and popular support appears relatively intact in these regions. In fact, according to a 2010 report issued by the Bogotá-based NGO New Rainbow Corporation (Corporación Nuevo Arco Iris), more soldiers and police were killed in each of the last two years (2009 and 2010) than at the height of the conflict in 2002.[3] However, there is a difference in the nature of these casualties. Most resulted from defensive actions by the FARC such as planting landmines, whereas ten years ago soldiers and police were being killed in large-scale guerrilla offensives launched against small and medium-sized towns. Nevertheless, the FARC continues to carry out offensive actions, conducting more than

1,800 attacks in 2010, albeit on a much smaller scale than in the past.[4] Furthermore, the overwhelming majority of these attacks were confined to the three regions in which the FARC maintains a strong presence rather than throughout the country.

As it has done throughout its history, the FARC has adapted to the shifting military conditions. The International Crisis Group noted in a March 2009 report that 'under its new leader, Alfonso Cano, the FARC has shown renewed internal cohesion and continued capacity to adapt to changes in the security environment.'[5] The report's reference to 'renewed internal cohesion' reflects Cano's efforts to address the concerns of Secretariat members over the previous decade that the guerrilla group had grown so fast that it was losing some of its ideological cohesion. Upon assuming command of the FARC, Cano quickly set about re-emphasizing political training among the group's rank-and-file members and reorganizing the FARC into a smaller, more disciplined and mobile military force utilizing conventional hit-and-run guerrilla tactics. This shift was evident in the weeks following the inauguration of newly elected President Juan Manuel Santos in August 2010 when the FARC launched a series of attacks that killed more than fifty soldiers and police.

The Dirty War Continues

Many analysts and the mainstream media have lauded the security successes of President Uribe and hailed Colombia as a shining example of democracy. Others have asked: security and democracy for whom? After all, the security situation has not improved for millions of Colombians, particularly those living in rural conflict zones. According to Jorge Rojas, director of the Bogotá-based Consultancy on Human Rights and Displacement (CODHES), 4.9 million Colombians have been forcibly displaced by violence in the past twenty-five years. However, 2.4 million of them were displaced during President Uribe's eight years in office (2002–10).[6] The Colombian military's aggressive counterinsurgency operations under Uribe's 'democratic security' strategy are a major cause of the country's escalating refugee crisis as soldiers forcibly displace communities in guerrilla-controlled zones. According to the Norwegian Refugee Council, 'The government's military strategy, which was intended to be preventive, is instead resulting in an increased displacement of people.'[7]

Meanwhile, the Colombian military's statistics on the number of guerrillas killed on the battlefield have been grossly inflated through the inclusion of civilians that were executed and then dressed up as rebels. The final year of Uribe's presidency was rocked by the 'false-positives' scandal, which revealed that impoverished young men were being recruited from the poor neighbourhoods of Colombia's cities and offered jobs in the countryside. Once they arrived at their destinations, the young men would be handed over to the Colombian army, executed and passed off as guerrillas killed in combat in order to boost body count numbers. Colombia's attorney general's office is investigating the extrajudicial execution by the military of more than two thousand civilians during Uribe's eight years in office.[8]

The Uribe administration has also been mired in other scandals that raise serious questions about the state of democracy in Colombia. Following the demobilization of the AUC paramilitary organization in 2006, the public prosecutor's office and the Supreme Court began investigating alleged links between elected officials and right-wing death squads. Two years later, sixty-nine members of Congress were under investigation for aiding, abetting and collaborating with paramilitaries. The overwhelming majority of the congressional representatives under investigation were Uribe's allies.[9] The Uribe administration did its best to derail the investigations, including extraditing fourteen high-ranking paramilitary leaders to the United States on drug-trafficking charges in an effort to prevent them from cooperating with Colombian investigators. The Uribe government also attempted to strip the Supreme Court of its constitutional responsibility for investigating lawmakers. Ultimately, the para-politics investigation confirmed claims made by former paramilitary commander Salvatore Mancuso in 2002 that the AUC controlled 35 per cent of Congress.[10]

It is not only Colombian politicians and the military that have colluded with the paramilitaries – so have multinational corporations. Numerous US companies including Occidental Petroleum, Drummond Mining and Coca-Cola are alleged to have maintained close ties with paramilitaries and have had to defend themselves in US federal court against accusations that they aided and abetted the AUC in its dirty war. In 2007, the relationship between multinationals and the death squads was made evident when Cincinnati-based Chiquita pleaded guilty in US federal court to funding AUC paramilitaries to protect the company's business interests in the banana-growing region in northern Colombia from guerrilla attacks. Chiquita admitted paying paramilitaries $1.7 million between 1997 and 2004, even though the company knew that the AUC was on the US State Department's list of foreign terrorist organizations. During the period that Chiquita was funding the AUC, the paramilitaries killed thousands of civilians in the banana-growing region. However, no criminal charges were ever brought against Chiquita executives and the company was only required to pay a $25 million fine for its transgressions.[11]

In 2009, yet another scandal broke in Colombia when it was revealed that the Department of Administrative Security (DAS), an intelligence agency that reports directly to the office

of the president, had been engaged in illegal wiretapping and
surveillance operations targeting political opponents, journalists,
civil society groups and Supreme Court justices. The DAS even
intercepted the emails of international organizations such as the
United Nations High Commissioner for Refugees, Human Rights
Watch, Peace Brigades International and the Washington Office
on Latin America. And in what the DAS named 'Operation
Europe', the intelligence agency monitored the email communications of European Union legislators.[12]

One of the Supreme Court justices under surveillance was Iván
Velásquez, the chief investigator in the para-politics scandal, who
had more than 1,900 of his phone calls recorded by DAS during
a three-month period. After the illegal surveillance operations
became public, one DAS investigator stated:

> Any person or entity who represents an eventual danger for the
> government has to be monitored by the DAS. As a result, more
> than a year ago, the activities of the [Supreme] Court, and some
> of its members, came to be considered and treated as a legitimate
> 'target'.[13]

In addition to the widespread repression and abuse of power
perpetrated by the government, very little of the wealth generated
by the country's much-lauded economic growth under neoliberalism trickled down to the poor. When Uribe assumed office in
2002, Colombia ranked 68th – one place above neighbouring
Venezuela – in the UN's Human Development Index, which
measures a country's quality of life based on life expectancy,
access to education and the average citizen's purchasing power.[14]
By 2009, Colombia had slipped to 77th on the Index while Venezuela had risen to 58th under President Hugo Chávez's distinctly
anti-neoliberal agenda.[15]

During the same period, while many of the region's left-
leaning governments achieved significant decreases in inequality,

Colombia experienced a widening in the gap between the rich and the poor.[16] Clearly, neoliberalism in Colombia has disproportionately benefited the wealthy classes and multinational corporations, which have taken advantage of favourable investment conditions and improved security in resource-rich regions. In all likelihood, a continuation of government repression and the poor socio-economic conditions experienced by many Colombians, particularly in rural regions, will only ensure a continued flow of recruits to the FARC – and a prolongation of the conflict.

A Political Solution?

The slaughter of the UP party during the late 1980s and early 1990s effectively exterminated the electoral left in Colombia for the next decade. But in July 2003, the centre-left Independent Democratic Pole (Polo Democrático Independiente, PDI) was formed to challenge the hegemony of the traditional political parties and immediately made an impact in municipal elections by winning Bogotá's mayoral race and the governorship of the department of Valle de Cauca. Prior to the 2006 elections, the PDI formed an alliance with another new centre-left party, the Democratic Alternative (AD), under the banner Alternative Democratic Pole (Polo Democrático Alternativo, PDA). The PDA's leadership primarily consisted of demobilized M-19 guerrillas, members of the Communist Party and unionists. Its presidential candidate, Carlos Gavíria, finished second – ahead of the Liberal Party candidate – in the 2006 election, garnering 22 per cent of the vote, the most ever for a left-of-centre candidate.

The PDA rejected armed struggle and sought a negotiated settlement to the armed conflict. It also emphasized the need to address the socio-economic causes of the violence. Some PDA members were openly critical of the FARC. Senator Gustavo

Petro, a former M-19 guerrilla, claimed that the guerrilla group's involvement in the coca trade

> caused changes in the attitude of the FARC, from being peasant guerrillas, revolutionaries of the old form; they became an army, like the paramilitaries, that grew because they could buy weapons and pay soldiers and mercenaries, and become militarily powerful.... They acquired control over territory, but in another way they lost, because their political ideology and their methods grew increasingly distant from society. They became more barbarous, carrying out actions that didn't even target the army but targeted the society in its entirety. They became isolated. They do not need the traditional support that traditional guerrillas need, because the money allows their army to be self-supporting and to expand. They do not need popular support, and they are losing their politics. Today, they are simply criminals.[17]

For many Colombians, the electoral successes of the PDA and the fact that its members have not been slaughtered illustrate that social justice in Colombia can finally be achieved through the ballot box. But the FARC has a different view of the PDA. When asked why the PDA is not being violently decimated like the UP, FARC commander Raúl Reyes explained:

> Inside the Pole there is the right, the social democrats and the left.... The social democrats have the largest presence in the Pole and they are taking advantage by trying to get to the presidency of the republic; to attain important positions inside the government, inside the state. Among these are several demobilized members of the M-19: Navarro, Gustavo Petro and others. Also, there are some who left the Communist Party to join the social democrats and they are proclaimed the 'democratic left'. These include Lucho Garzón and Angelino Garzón, among others. These people have accepted the establishment, the state, because they calculate, and it's a mis-calculation, that they will be able to attract the revolutionary left. But it so happens that the revolutionary left cannot be attracted to the social democrats because we are conscious that social democrats

end up favouring the right, the bourgeoisie.... It so happens that the commitment is not to the people; the commitment is to fight for new possibilities to attain positions inside the government. However, within the Pole, some continue to fight to maintain it a little towards the left. They say that if the Pole cannot be maintained towards the left then later they are not going to be able to differentiate between the Liberal Party and the Pole. But it is going to be a very difficult fight. I believe that for all these reasons, the Colombian state has not used the force, has not had the disposition to commit the assassinations, that it did in the past. Nevertheless, it should be noted that they do continue murdering people, but they are selective murders of the people that truly are on the left. These people are union leaders, peasant leaders and teachers who are engaged in the struggle on behalf of the people.[18]

And thus the FARC justifies its continuation of the armed struggle. In the eyes of the FARC, the PDA constitutes a reform party that will not seriously challenge the fundamental structures of capitalism or the state; it is not a revolutionary political movement like the UP, and so the state and the paramilitaries are not particularly threatened by its existence and its electoral successes.

Another reason that might explain the fact that the PDA has been targeted to a much lesser degree than the UP was offered by Carlos Castaño, commander-in-chief of the AUC until his death in 2004. Reflecting on the UP, Castaño suggested that the paramilitaries had erred in their slaughter of the party's members:

The ignorance was so much for us that anything that looked like a guerrilla, anything that seemed from the left, and anything that was communist, was for us the same thing, including unions. This was our biggest mistake. If we had the slightest education that taught us at least what the democratic left was, what the radical left was, what communism was, what the FARC was, what the ELN was, what Maoism was, we wouldn't have committed so many mistakes and maybe we would be a legal 'self-defense' group today. But the ignorance was so much that whatever was on the Left was [part of] the same thing.[19]

In essence, Castaño's analysis closely reflects that offered by Reyes in that he appears to suggest that the Colombian right could coexist with a moderate left, perhaps along the lines of the PDA. One can only assume that Castaño came to this conclusion because he, as did Reyes, believed that a centre-left party did not pose a significant threat to the interests of the wealthy classes. A more selective assassination of those Colombians on the hard left, as Reyes pointed out, has continued, suggesting that a truly revolutionary leftist, or socialist, party would still not be tolerated by the country's elites.

Ultimately, Reyes's analysis of the PDA proved truly prescient. In the run-up to the 2010 elections, sectors within the PDA proposed forming an electoral alliance with the Liberal Party in order to oust Uribe from the presidency, thereby realizing Reyes's prediction from two years earlier that one day people 'are not going to be able to differentiate between the Liberal Party and the Pole'. Ultimately, fundamental differences between moderate and more leftist factions of the PDA led to a split in the party and a poor showing in the 2010 elections. Meanwhile, Reyes's claim that moderate, or social-democratic, members of the PDA, such as Angelino Garzón, were primarily interested in attaining high government positions was validated when Garzón became vice president under Uribe's hand-picked successor, President Juan Manuel Santos.

While independent parties and candidates, including Uribe, successfully shattered the stranglehold that the Liberal and Conservative parties had over Colombia's political affairs, there remains no evidence that a party palatable to the FARC and those on the non-violent left will achieve power – or even be permitted to exist – in the foreseeable future. This reality greatly diminishes the possibility of achieving a negotiated settlement to the conflict. The fact that security trumps economics as an election issue for many Colombians has helped the country buck the regional trend to the left at the polls and, ironically, will likely ensure a continuation of the conflict in one form or another.

Many on the non-violent left argue that the FARC's continued commitment to armed struggle provides the government with a convenient justification for its repression of those sectors of society that are peacefully and democratically struggling for peace and social justice. Even Venezuelan President Hugo Chávez shifted his stance in 2010, publicly calling for FARC guerrillas to lay down their weapons and demobilize because 'they have become an excuse for the [U.S.] empire to intervene in Colombia'.[20] But peace accords during the 1990s that led to the demobilization of the FMLN and other Central American guerrilla groups – and also the M-19 in Colombia – failed to address the social inequalities and injustices that lay at the root of those conflicts.

Ultimately, the legacy of the Central American peace accords consists of poverty, inequality and rampant gang and criminal violence. In essence, politically motivated violence has been replaced by a criminal violence marked by random and anarchic tendencies that is perpetrated by individuals and gangs. In Colombia, demobilized paramilitaries and guerrillas lose their government benefits three years after laying down their arms. But many of them do not have jobs because, as one demobilized FARC guerrilla noted, 'The doors of businesses are shut to us. They ask for my *cedula* [government-issued identification card] and check with the police, and when they find out that I'm a demobilized fighter they are afraid to hire me.'[21] According to Luís Fernando Martinez, who works with the demobilization programme, 'Because they cannot find work and have difficulty adapting to urban life, many of the demobilized are turning to crime or joining emergent criminal gangs.'[22] The increases in violent crime in Colombia's cities that have occurred since 2008 suggest that the shifting nature of violence evident in Central America following the armed conflicts in that region might well be occurring in Colombia.[23]

Some analysts point to the electoral success of the FMLN, which won the presidency of El Salvador in 2009, as an example of the potential for armed groups that demobilize and engage in the political process. But the FMLN's ideology is far more moderate today than when it was founded thirty years ago. As a result, it more closely reflects the social-democratic views of the PDA than the socialism it used to espouse, and, as is evident in Colombia, the right in El Salvador and the United States are willing to tolerate centre-left regimes that do not pose a significant threat to the fundamental structures of capitalism. Ultimately, a decade of escalated US military intervention in El Salvador led to a stalemate in that country's civil conflict and the eventual demobilization of the FMLN without any significant structural changes. Similarly, a decade of US military intervention under Plan Colombia has turned the tide in the Colombian conflict. However, as was the case in El Salvador, any peace agreement in Colombia that does not result in significant structural changes will also fail to achieve peace with social justice.

The United States is another factor ensuring the continuation of the Colombian conflict. Given the emergence of left-leaning governments throughout much of South America over the past decade, Colombia has become vitally important to the United States from a geopolitical perspective. The arrival of President Barack Obama in the White House has done little to change US policy towards Colombia. And to the degree that there has been a shift, it has been in the direction of increased militarization. The Obama administration has maintained the same high levels

of military aid to Colombia as that provided by both Bush and
Clinton governments. Additionally, the Obama administration
signed a ten-year base-sharing agreement with the Uribe government in October 2009 that will provide the US military with
access to seven military bases in Colombia.[24]

The regional security concerns of Colombia's neighbours,
particularly Venezuela's President Hugo Chávez and Bolivia's
President Evo Morales, over the base agreement appeared to
be validated when a US Air Force document addressing the
importance of gaining access to Colombia's Palenquero Air Base
was made public. According to the document, the Palenquero Air
Base 'provides a unique opportunity for full spectrum operations
in a critical sub region of our hemisphere where security and
stability is under constant threat from narcotics funded insurgencies, anti-US governments, endemic poverty and recurring
natural disasters'.[25] Clearly, the United States views Colombia
as geopolitically crucial to the furtherance of its own political,
economic and military objectives in the region.

Conclusion

Like most armed movements, the FARC is a complex organization. It has significant popular support in some rural regions of
Colombia and virtually none in others. It utilizes terrorist tactics
and perpetrates gross violations of human rights. It also profits
from the illicit drug trade. But simply to dismiss the FARC as a
criminal organization would be disingenuous. While many do not
agree with the FARC's ideology, or the strategy and tactics that
the guerrilla group has employed, the FARC is, nevertheless, a
political-military organization; it is ideologically motivated – and
labelling it as a terrorist organization is a tacit acknowledgement
of that fact. The FARC's ideology is firmly rooted in Marxism,

but a Marxism that is influenced by the Colombian reality, particularly the country's rural reality. As FARC commanders Iván Ríos and Fernando Caicedo noted in a joint communiqué:

> We believe that it is from the basis of the principles set out by Marx, without taking them as schemes or formulas or completely fashioned doctrines but as guides ... that the model for Colombian reality will have to emerge.... We speak of socialist revolution. If it will be communist or not is a question to be decided later on. The name we will give it is not of the least importance; the most important thing is that we agree that we need a new country.[26]

A videotaped message from the FARC's commander-in-chief Alfonso Cano, released just prior to the inauguration of Uribe's successor, President Santos, announced that the guerrilla group was willing to engage in peace talks so long as the neoliberal economic model, agrarian reform and US military intervention in Colombia were the principal points of negotiation.[27] President Santos, however, responded by demanding that the FARC unilaterally cease all armed actions and vowed to continue his predecessor's security and neoliberal economic policies.

A political solution to the armed conflict is unlikely to occur as long as the government insists that the only issues open for negotiation are the logistical questions related to the guerrilla group's demobilization. Any political solution must address the root causes of the conflict: the country's gross social and economic inequalities. After all, it is not only the FARC that is seeking such a transformation, but also millions of Colombians on the non-violent left.

Ultimately, if there is little or no change in the repressive security and economic policies implemented by the state, then the FARC will remain committed to armed struggle. According to Reyes, who spent twenty-six years fighting in the Colombian jungles before being killed by the military in March 2008,

We are motivated to wage the revolutionary struggle. We are motivated to support actions by the popular masses, protests by the
unions, by organizations, and likewise guerrilla actions. And this
is what we call 'the combination of all forms of struggle', because
the FARC is a revolutionary army and it does not only engage in the
armed struggle. The FARC is characterized as a political-military
organization. Its leadership is a political cell. All of the FARC is a
political cell. Therefore, its work involves the formation of guerrillas
who are strong both politically and ideologically so that they understand it is a fight for the structural changes that the country requires
and not for the benefit of certain people.[28]

In the two hundred years since Colombia declared independence, God remained true to his word with regard to the politicians
he intended to bestow upon the country. As a result, government
after government has refused to address effectively the root causes
of the conflict, with the tragic consequences being a continuation
of the violence into the twenty-first century. Colombia's rugged
mountains and vast expanses of jungle make the country an ideal
place for waging guerrilla warfare. The same geographical fea-
tures have resulted in a decentralized nation in which significant
political and economic power is dispersed among the country's
largest cities – Bogotá, Medellín, Cali and Barranquilla – which
are scattered across the national territory. Consequently, even if a
guerrilla army succeeded in seizing the capital, Bogotá, it would
not necessarily mean that the rebels would control the nation.
Therefore the very terrain that makes Colombia ideal for waging
guerrilla warfare also makes it difficult to win the war.

Meanwhile, US aid has dramatically improved the Colombian
military's intelligence-gathering capabilities and its capacity to
deploy rapidly well-trained combat units by helicopter, thereby
putting the FARC on the defensive. But the country's geography
continues to pose huge challenges for the military, despite its
technological superiority, in its effort to defeat the insurgency

in its traditional strongholds. According to Lieutenant Colonel Rodolfo Mantilla, commander of the Caicedo Battalion, which operates in the rugged mountains of south-central Colombia where FARC leader Alfonso Cano is based, 'There has been a lot of blood spilled in these mountains, by our soldiers and by the guerrillas. This is not a mission that can be accomplished in weeks, or in months. It is going to take years.'[29]

How the FARC continues to adapt to the shifting military terrain will likely determine the nature of the conflict in the years ahead. If the FARC has proven one thing over the decades it is its ability to adapt and to survive. Consequently, there is a real possibility that the FARC will continue its armed struggle for many more years. But even if the military continues to have success on the battlefield and ultimately defeats the FARC, the demobilization of the guerrillas will not likely end the violence in Colombia. Unless far-reaching structural changes are implemented that address Colombia's gross social and economic inequalities, the violence in one form or another will likely continue deep into the twenty-first century.

Notes

CHAPTER 1

1. James E. Sanders, *Contentious Republicans: Popular Politics, Race, and Class in Nineteenth-Century Colombia* (Durham, NC: Duke University Press, 2004), pp. 159–60.
2. In reality, the law not only failed to alleviate the inequitable distribution of land, it actually sanctioned the property claims of many large landowners. See Catherine LeGrand, 'Agrarian Antecedents of the Violence', in Charles Bergquist, Ricardo Pendaranda and Gonzalo Sanchez (eds), *Violence in Colombia: The Contemporary Crisis in Historical Perspective* (Wilmington, DE: Scholarly Resources, 1992), p. 42.
3. Robert W. Drexler, *Colombia and the United States: Narcotics Traffic and a Failed Foreign Policy* (Jefferson, NC: McFarland, 1997), p. 62.
4. Ernesto 'Che' Guevara, *The Motorcycle Diaries: A Journey Around South America* (London: Verso, 1995), p. 144.
5. Manuel Marulanda Vélez, 'The Origins of the FARC–EP: The Birth of Armed Resistance', in Rebeca Toledo, Teresa Gutierrez, Sara Flounders and Andy McInerny (eds), *War in Colombia: Made in U.S.A* (New York: International Action Center, 2003), p. 117.
6. Gonzalo Sánchez, 'The Violence: An Interpretive Synthesis', in Charles Bergquist, Ricardo Peñaranda and Gonzalo Sánchez (eds), *Violence in Colombia: The Contemporary Crisis in Historical Perspective* (Wilmington, DE: Scholarly Resources, 1992), p. 93.
7. Revolutionary Armed Forces of Colombia – People's Army (FARC–EP), *FARC–EP: Historical Outline* (Toronto: International Commission, Revolutionary Armed Forces of Colombia – People's Army, 1999), p. 15.
8. Camilo Torres, 'Violence and Socio-Cultural Change in Rural Colombia',

in M. Zeitlin (ed.), *Father Camilo Torres: Revolutionary Writings* (New York: Harper Colophon Books, 1969), p. 132.

9. Ibid., p. 174.
10. Marco Palacios, *Between Legitimacy and Violence: A History of Colombia, 1875–2002* (Durham, NC: Duke University Press, 2006), p. 166.
11. James J. Brittain, *Revolutionary Social Change in Colombia: The Origin and Direction of the FARC-EP* (London: Pluto Press, 2010), p. 14.
12. Dennis M. Rempe, 'Guerrillas, Bandits, and Independent Republics: US Counter-Insurgency Efforts in Colombia, 1959–1965', *Small Wars and Insurgencies*, Winter 1995.
13. Torres, 'Violence and Socio-Cultural Change in Rural Colombia', p. 178.
14. FARC-EP, *FARC-EP: Historical Outline*, p. 22.
15. Marulanda Vélez, 'The Origins of the FARC-EP: The Birth of Armed Resistance', p. 120.
16. Ibid., pp. 120–22.
17. Major Jon-Paul Maddaloni, 'An Analysis of the FARC in Colombia: Breaking the Frame of FM 3-24', School of Advanced Military Studies, US Army, 2009.
18. Palacios, *Between Legitimacy and Violence*, p. 193.
19. Ibid., p. 193.
20. Ibid., p. 266.
21. Eduardo Pizarro, 'Revolutionary Guerrilla Groups in Colombia', in Bergquist et al. (eds), *Violence in Colombia*, p. 181.
22. Frank Safford and Marco Palacios, *Colombia: Fragmented Land, Divided Society* (New York: Oxford University Press, 2002), p. 356.
23. Drexler, *Colombia and the United States*, pp. 82–3.
24. Safford and Palacios, *Colombia: Fragmented Land, Divided Society*, p. 309.
25. Nazih Richani, *Systems of Violence: The Political Economy of War and Peace in Colombia* (Albany, NY: State University of New York Press, 2002), p. 28.
26. Ibid., p. 28.
27. Alfredo Molano, 'Violence and Land Colonization', in Bergquist et al. (eds), *Violence in Colombia*, p. 206.
28. FARC-EP, *FARC-EP: Historical Outline*, p. 117. The original agrarian reform programme was revised in 1993 and it is the revised version that is referred to here.
29. Ibid., p. 117.
30. Ibid., p. 118.
31. Ibid., pp. 118–19.
32. Molano, 'Violence and Land Colonization', p. 207.
33. Alfredo Molano, 'The Evolution of the FARC: A Guerrilla Group's Long History', *NACLA Report on the Americas*, September/October 2000.
34. Drexler, *Colombia and the United States*, p. 112.
35. Ibid.

36. Maddaloni, 'An Analysis of the FARC in Colombia'.
37. Palacios, *Between Legitimacy and Violence*, p. 266.
38. Brittain, *Revolutionary Social Change in Colombia*, p. 59.
39. Ibid., p. 48.

CHAPTER 2

1. Revolutionary Armed Forces of Colombia – People's Army (FARC-EP), *FARC-EP: Historical Outline* (Toronto: International Commission, Revolutionary Armed Forces of Colombia – People's Army, 1999), p. 26.
2. Ricardo Vargas Meza, 'The FARC, the War, and the Crisis of State', *NACLA Report on the Americas*, March/April 1998, p. 24.
3. Steven Dudley, *Walking Ghosts: Murder and Guerrilla Politics in Colombia* (New York: Routledge, 2006), p. 60.
4. Ibid., pp. 62–4.
5. Ibid., pp. 91–2.
6. Commission for the Study of Violence, 'Organized Violence', in Charles Bergquist, Ricardo Peñaranda and Gonzalo Sánchez (eds), *Violence in Colombia: The Contemporary Crisis in Historical Perspective* (Wilmington, DE: Scholarly Resources, 1992), p. 268.
7. Human Rights Watch, *Colombia's Killer Networks: The Military-Paramilitary Partnership and the United States* (New York: Human Rights Watch, 1996), p.17.
8. Dudley, *Walking Ghosts*, p. 43.
9. FARC-EP, *FARC-EP: Historical Outline*, p. 49.
10. Dudley, *Walking Ghosts*, p. 83.
11. Ibid., p. 128.
12. 'Piden vincular a ex jefe de inteligencia del DAS con el magnicidio de Bernardo Jaramillo', *El Tiempo*, 11 February 2010.
13. The Simón Bolívar Guerrilla Coordinating Committee (Coordinadora Guerrillera Simón Bolívar, CGSB) was named after independence hero Simón Bolívar, who liberated much of South America from Spanish rule in the early 1800s.
14. Alfredo Molano, 'The Evolution of the FARC: A Guerrilla Group's Long History', *NACLA Report on the Americas*, September/October 2000.
15. FARC-EP, *FARC-EP: Historical Outline*, p. 36.
16. Robert W. Drexler, *Colombia and the United States: Narcotics Traffic and a Failed Foreign Policy* (Jefferson, NC: McFarland, 1997), p. 165.
17. FARC-EP, *FARC-EP: Historical Outline*, pp. 39–40.
18. Nazih Richani, *Systems of Violence: The Political Economy of War and Peace in Colombia* (Albany, NY: State University of New York Press, 2002), p. 65.
19. Simón Trinidad, interview with author, Los Pozos, Caquetá, Colombia, 14 June 2000.

CHAPTER 3

1. Benjamin Keen, *A History of Latin America* (Boston, MA: Houghton Mifflin, 1996), p. 514.
2. Nazih Richani, *Systems of Violence: The Political Economy of War and Peace in Colombia* (Albany, NY: State University of New York Press, 2002), p. 70.
3. Revolutionary Armed Forces of Colombia – People's Army (FARC–EP), *FARC–EP: Historical Outline* (Toronto: International Commission, Revolutionary Armed Forces of Colombia – People's Army, 1999), p. 91.
4. Luis Enrique Gonzalez, 'Interview with FARC's Raul Reyes', *Prensa Latina*, 20 July 2001.
5. James J. Brittain, *Revolutionary Social Change in Colombia: The Origin and Direction of the FARC–EP* (London: Pluto Press, 2010), pp. 100–101.
6. Scott Wilson, 'Colombia's Rebel Zone: World Apart', *Washington Post*, 18 October 2003.
7. Ibid.
8. Brittain, *Revolutionary Social Change in Colombia*, p. 168.
9. Based on author's observations and interviews with residents during visits to La Cooperativa in Meta, Colombia, in August 2006 and February 2009.
10. Ibid.
11. Richani, *Systems of Violence*, p. 80.
12. Ibid., p. 70.
13. Anonymous, interview with author, San Vicente del Caguán, Caquetá, Colombia, 15 June 2000.
14. Anonymous, interview with author, El Tigre, Meta, Colombia, 17 August 2006.
15. Wilson, 'Colombia's Rebel Zone'.
16. Simón Trinidad, interview with author, Los Pozos, Caquetá, Colombia, 14 June 2000.
17. Brittain, *Revolutionary Social Change in Colombia*, p. 113.
18. Ibid., p. 138.
19. Ibid., pp. 155–6.
20. 'The Peace Community of San José de Apartadó: Communities in Resistance in Colombia', Amnesty International, March 2009.
21. Gary Marx, 'Fighting Impunity in Colombia', *Chicago Tribune*, 1 April 2007.
22. Kirsten Begg, 'Congressman Takes Case against Uribe to ICC', *Colombia Reports*, 18 August 2010.
23. Hannah Stone, 'Soldiers Acquitted of Peace Community Massacre', 9 August 2010.
24. Erika, interview with author, Los Pozos, Caquetá, Colombia, 27 January 2001.
25. Ibid.

26. Jon, interview with author, Ibagué, Tolima, Colombia, 15 December 2010.

27. Miriam Narváez, interview by Terry Gibbs, Putumayo, Colombia, June 2007.

28. Primarily based on author's observations and interviews during a three-day visit to a FARC camp in Putumayo, Colombia, in June 2007.

29. Gladys Marín, interview by Terry Gibbs, Putumayo, Colombia, June 2007.

30. Pandora Pugsley, 'FARC Leader's Female Guerrilla Team', *Colombia Reports*, 21 July 2010.

31. Terry Gibbs, 'Voices from the Colombian Left: Women and the Struggle for Social Transformation', *Labour, Capital and Class*, 2011.

32. Ibid.

33. Jeanie Gong, 'FARC – Rebels with a Cause?', Council on Hemispheric Affairs, 6 July 2010.

34. Lucero, interview with author, San Vicente del Caguán, Caquetá, Colombia, 16 June 2000.

35. Anonymous, interview with author, Putumayo, Colombia, June 2007.

36. Carlos Villalón, 'Cocaine Country', *National Geographic*, July 2004.

37. Kirsten Begg, 'Colombian Army Destroys FARC Hospital', *Colombia Reports*, 12 February 2010.

38. Ibid.

CHAPTER 4

1. Mark Chernik, 'The Paramilitarization of the War in Colombia', *NACLA Report on the Americas*, March/April 1998, p. 30.

2. Human Rights Watch, *Colombia's Killer Networks*, p. 25.

3. Ibid., pp. 23–4.

4. Patrick L. Clawson and Rensselear W. Lee III, *The Andean Cocaine Industry* (New York: St. Martin's Press, 1998), p. 52.

5. 'Fact Sheet: Colombia, U.N. Discussing Anti Coca Mycoherbicide Cooperation', US Department of State, 17 July 2000.

6. Nazih Richani, *Systems of Violence: The Political Economy of War and Peace in Colombia* (Albany, NY: State University of New York Press, 2002), p. 72.

7. Alfredo Molano, 'Violence and Land Colonization', in Charles Bergquist, Ricardo Peñaranda and Gonzalo Sánchez (eds), *Violence in Colombia: The Contemporary Crisis in Historical Perspective* (Wilmington, DE: Scholarly Resources, 1992), p. 215.

8. Ibid.

9. Richani, *Systems of Violence*, p. 75.

10. Chernik, 'The Paramilitarization of the War in Colombia', p. 32.

11. Molano, 'Violence and Land Colonization', p. 214.

12. Alfredo Molano, 'The Evolution of the FARC': A Guerrilla Group's Long

History', *NACLA Report on the Americas*, September/October 2000.

13. Francisco E. Thoumi, *Illegal Drugs, Economy, and Society in the Andes* (Baltimore: Johns Hopkins University Press, 2003), p. 104.

14. Oscar Jansson, interview with author, Uppsala, Sweden, 16 November 2006.

15. Thoumi, *Illegal Drugs, Economy, and Society in the Andes*, p. 107.

16. Ibid., pp. 106–7.

17. Russell Crandall, *Driven by Drugs: U.S. Policy Toward Colombia* (Boulder, CO: Lynne Rienner, 2002), p. 91.

18. Simón Trinidad, interview with author, Los Pozos, Caquetá, Colombia, 14 June 2000.

19. James J. Brittain, *Revolutionary Social Change in Colombia: The Origin and Direction of the FARC-EP* (London: Pluto Press, 2010), pp. 91–2; emphasis in original.

20. Major Jon-Paul Maddaloni, 'An Analysis of the FARC in Colombia: Breaking the Frame of FM 3–24', School of Advanced Military Studies, US Army, 2009.

21. Doug Stokes, *America's Other War: Terrorizing Colombia* (London: Zed Books, 2005), p. 102.

22. Brittain, *Revolutionary Social Change in Colombia*, pp. 96–7.

23. Forrest Hylton, *Evil Hour in Colombia* (London: Verso, 2006), p. 101.

24. Bert Ruiz, *The Colombian Civil War* (Jefferson, NC: McFarland, 2001), p. 21.

25. 'Multilateral Invasion Force for Colombia?', *NACLA Report on the Americas*, May/June 1998, pp. 46–7.

26. Stan Goff, 'Is Colombia the Next Vietnam?, Workers World News Service, 30 July 2002.

27. Donnie Marshall, 'DEA Congressional Testimony', Subcommittee on National Security, International Affairs and Criminal Justice, 9 July 1997.

28. Winifred Tate, 'Colombia's Role in International Drug Industry', *Foreign Policy in Focus*, 1 November 1999.

29. Associated Press, 'UN Envoy Triggers a Debate in Colombia', *Daily Mail*, 22 May 2003.

30. 'FARC Fact Sheet', US Drug Enforcement Administration, 22 March 2006.

31. 'United States Charges 50 Leaders of Narco-Terrorist FARC in Colombia with Supplying More than Half of the World's Cocaine', US Drug Enforcement Administration, 22 March 2006.

32. Paul Wolf, 'Autopsy of a Narco-Guerrillera', *WW4 Report*, 1 March 2007.

33. Ibid.

34. Ibid.

35. Ayse M. Weiting, 'Colombian Drug Trafficker Gets 27 Years', FOX News, 22 July 2010.

36. Jon, interview with author, Ibagué, Tolima, Colombia, 15 December 2010.

37. Samuel Logan, 'FARC's Revolution is Over', International Relations and Security Network, 7 July 2008.
38. 'Las Farc por dentro', *Semana*, 28 November 2009.

CHAPTER 5

1. Mario A. Murillo, *Colombia and the United States: War, Unrest and Destabilization* (New York: Seven Stories Press, 2004), p. 98.
2. Anonymous, interview with author, San Vicente del Caguán, Caquetá, Colombia, 28 January 2001.
3. Father Miguel Serna, interview with author, San Vicente del Caguán, Caquetá, Colombia, 15 June 2000.
4. George H.W. Bush, 'Statement on Trade Initiatives for the Andean Region', George Bush Presidential Library and Museum, 1 November 1989.
5. 'Colombia Poverty Report', World Bank Group, March 2002.
6. Revolutionary Armed Forces of Colombia – People's Army (FARC-EP), *FARC-EP: Historical Outline* (Toronto: International Commission, Revolutionary Armed Forces of Colombia – People's Army, 1999), p. 130.
7. Peter Dale Scott, *Drugs, Oil and War: The United States in Afghanistan, Colombia and Indochina* (Lanham, MA: Rowman & Littlefield, 2003), p. 74.
8. Iván Ríos, interview with author, San Vicente del Caguán, Caquetá, Colombia, 30 January 2001.
9. Francisco Ramírez Cuellar, *The Profits of Extermination: How U.S. Corporate Power is Destroying Colombia* (Monroe, ME: Common Courage Press, 2005), p. 32.
10. Dr Edgar Perea, interview with author, La Hormiga, Putumayo, Colombia, 10 February 2001. Also, author witnessed food crops destroyed by aerial fumigations in Putumayo.
11. Jair Giovani Ruiz, interview with author, Puerto Asís, Putumayo, Colombia, 20 August 2002.
12. Mario Cabal, interview with author, Puerto Asís, Putumayo, Colombia, 20 August 2002.
13. Doctor Ruben Dario Pinzón, interview with author, Puerto Asís, Putumayo, Colombia, 6 February 2001.
14. Victoriano, interview with author, Putumayo, Colombia, 19 August 2002.
15. Cecilia, interview with author, Meta, Colombia, 17 August 2006.
16. Anonymous, interview with author, Meta, Colombia, 17 August 2006.
17. Indira A.R. Lakshmanan, '$4 Billion Later, Drugs Still Flow in Colombia', *Boston Globe*, 21 May 2006.
18. 'US Blames Colombia Rebels for Peace Talks Collapse', Reuters, 19 July 1999.
19. Doug Stokes, *America's Other War: Terrorizing Colombia* (London: Zed Books, 2005), p. 96.
20. Bert Ruiz, *The Colombian Civil War* (Jefferson: McFarland, 2001), p. 64.

21. Ingrid Vaicius and Adam Isacson, 'The "War on Drugs" meets the "War on Terror"', Center for International Policy, February 2003.
22. Ibid.
23. 'Testimony of Francis X. Taylor, Coordinator of Counterterrorism', House Committee on International Relations, US House of Representatives, 10 October 2001.
24. Secretary Colin L. Powell, 'Testimony on the International Campaign Against Terrorism', Senate Foreign Relations Committee, US Senate, 25 October 2001.
25. Senator Bob Graham, 'Excerpt from press conference with Sen. Bob Graham (D–Florida)', Center for International Policy, 25 October 2001.
26. 'Supplemental Aid for 2002', Center for International Policy, 1 August 2003.
27. General James Hill, 'Regarding U.S. Narcotics Policy in Colombia', Senate Caucus on International Narcotics Control, US Senate, 3 June 2003.
28. 'The Effectiveness of the Colombian Democratic Security and Defence Policy', Colombian Ministry of Defence, August 2003.
29. 'Alerta frente a las cifras gobernamentales sobre derechos humanos en Colombia', Comisión Colombiana de Juristas, 4 July 2003. See also 'The Effectiveness of the Colombian Democratic Security and Defence Policy', Colombian Ministry of Defence, August 2003.
30. 'A Laboratory of War: Repression and Violence in Arauca', Amnesty International, 20 April 2004.
31. 'Colombia: Rights Defenders Under Attack', Inter Press Service, 1 September 2003.
32. 'Colombia: En contravía de las recomendaciones internacionales sobre derechos humanos, Balance de la política de seguridad democrática y la situación de derechos humanos y derecho humanitario, agosto 2002 a agosto 2004', Comisión Colombiana de Juristas, 15 October 2004.
33. 'Colombia: Rights Defenders Under Attack', Inter Press Service.
34. Amaranta Wright, 'In Colombia's Jungles, Echoes of Argentina's "Disappeared"', San Francisco Chronicle, 12 January 2004.
35. 'UN Urges Colombia Rights Action', BBC News, 14 July 2005.
36. Wright, 'In Colombia's Jungles, Echoes of Argentina's "Disappeared"'. See also Alfredo Castro, 'Colombia's Disappeared: 25 People a Week Go Missing', Counterpunch, 29 July 2002.
37. 'El Embrujo Autoritario: Primer Año de Gobierno de Álvaro Uribe Vélez', Plataforma Colombiana de Derechos Humanos, Democracia y Desarrollo, September 2003.
38. President Alvaro Uribe, 'Palabras del Presidente Uribe en posesión de nuevo comandante de la FAC', Presidencia de la Republica, 8 September 2003.
39. President Alvaro Uribe, 'Discurso del Presidente Uribe en la Asamblea de Naciones Unidas', Presidencia de la Republica, 30 September 2003. See also US Secretary Colin L. Powell, 'Remarks after Meeting with Colombian

President Alvaro Uribe', US Department of State, 30 September 2003.
40. Commander Enrique, interview with author, 7 February 2001, La Hormiga, Putumayo, Colombia.
41. Secretary Colin Powell, 'Press Conference from Bogotá', US Department of State, 4 December 2002.
42. Phil Stewart, 'Oil Declining, Colombia Offers New Deal in Houston', Reuters, 9 March 2004.
43. Lieutenant Colonel Francisco Javier Cruz, interview with author, 2 March 2004, Orito, Putumayo, Colombia.
44. Ibid.
45. Spokesperson for Occidental Petroleum, interview with author, 10 February 2003, Bogotá, Colombia.
46. 'The Real Costs of Pipeline Protection in Arauca: Corporate Welfare with Deadly Consequences', Witness for Peace, July 2002. Witness for Peace's $3.70 per barrel figure was based on the $98 million in aid requested by the Bush administration. Congress only approved $93 million, which brought the cost of subsidization down to $3.55 per barrel.
47. 'Protecting the Pipeline: The US Military Mission Expands', Washington Office on Latin America, May 2003.
48. Brigadier General Carlos Lemus, interview with author, 9 August 2002, Arauca City, Arauca, Colombia.
49. Gary Marx, 'Imperiled Pipeline Gets US Troops in Colombia', *Chicago Tribune*, 12 November 2002.
50. 'Possible Disappearance: Colombia Indigenous and Peasant Farmer Communities in Tame Municipality, Department of Arauca', Amnesty International, 3 June 2003.
51. *Amnesty International Report 2004*, Amnesty International, 26 May 2004.
52. Anonymous US Army Special Forces soldier, interview with author, 5 February 2003, Saravena, Arauca, Colombia.
53. 'Colombia: Trade Unionists and Human Rights Defenders Under Attack', Amnesty International, 27 August 2003.
54. 'Colombia: Mass Arrests of Politicians', Associated Press, 22 October 2003.
55. '25 Colombians Suspected of Rebel Ties', Associated Press, 21 October 2003.
56. Juan Forero, 'Bogotá Says Army Killed Union Chiefs', *New York Times*, 8 September 2004.
57. T. Christian Miller, 'US Troops Answered Oil Firms Pleas', *Los Angeles Times*, 30 December 2004.
58. 'Patterns of Global Terrorism 2000', US Department of State, 30 April 2001.
59. 'Country Reports on Terrorism 2009', US Department of State, 5 August 2010.
60. Noam Chomsky, *Power and Terror: Post-9/11 Talks and Interviews* (New York: Seven Stories Press, 2003), p. 60.

61. Patrick J. O'Donoghue, 'UN Advisor Snubs USA … "FARC Is NOT a Terrorist Group"', *VHeadline*, 19 May 2003.
62. Paul Wolf, 'FARC Is Not a Terrorist Group', *Colombia Journal*, 14 January 2008.
63. Ibid.
64. Kiraz Janicke, 'Venezuelan Legislature Supports Belligerent Status for Colombian Rebels', *Venezuela Analysis*, 18 January 2008.
65. Helen Murphy and Mathew Walter, 'Chávez Calls FARC a "Real Army" Worthy of Respect', Bloomberg, 11 January 2008.
66. Pablo Bachelet, 'U.S. May Add Venezuela to List of Terrorist States', McClatchy Newspapers, 10 March 2008.
67. Ewen Allison and Robert K. Goldman, 'Belligerent Status', in Roy Gutman and David Rieff, *Crimes of War: What the Public Should Know* (New York: W.W. Norton, 1999), p. 42.

CHAPTER 6

1. The author has repeatedly heard such claims in interviews with many Colombians from all walks of life. Such claims have also been widely stated in the media.
2. 'Annual Report of the Inter-American Commission on Human Rights 1999', Organization of American States, 13 April 2000.
3. Ibid.
4. *World Report 2000*, Human Rights Watch, December 1999.
5. 'Country Report on Human Rights Practices 1999', US Department of State, 23 February 2000.
6. Ibid.
7. Ambassador Curtis W. Kamman, 'Paramilitaries Massacre as Many as 50 in Norte de Santander', National Security Archive, 16 October 2005.
8. US Department of Defense, 'FARC Guerrilla Commanders and Paramilitary Group Members Comment on Their Organizations and Activities', National Security Archive, 16 October 2005.
9. Central Intelligence Agency, 'Senior Executive Intelligence Brief', National Security Archive, 16 October 2005.
10. Human Rights Watch, *The 'Sixth Division': Military–Paramilitary Ties and U.S. Policy in Colombia* (New York: Human Rights Watch, 2001), p. 22.
11. Ibid.
12. R. Nicholas Burns, 'Promoting Peace and Prosperity in Colombia', US State Department, 22 October 2007.
13. Garry Leech, 'Bloody Foundation for U.S.–Colombia Free Trade Agreement', *Beacon Broadside*, 30 April 2008.
14. 'Annual Survey of Violations of Trade Union Rights 2009', International Trade Union Confederation, June 2009.
15. *World Report 2000*.

16. Kevin Whitelaw, 'Inside Colombia's War on Kidnapping', *US News & World Report*, 27 February 2008.
17. 'Estadisticas secuestro a 2006', Fundación País Libre, 2007.
18. 'FARC Admits Coca Farmers Massacre', BBC News, 18 June 2004.
19. Rick Kearns, 'FARC Massacre of Indigenous in Columbia, More Deaths and Displacement', *Indian Country Today*, 13 March 2009.
20. Simón Trinidad, interview with author, Los Pozos, Caquetá, Colombia, 14 June 2000.
21. 'You'll Learn Not to Cry: Child Combatants in Colombia', Human Rights Watch, September 2003.
22. Ibid.
23. Gabriel Elizondo, 'Recruiting Children in Colombia', Al Jazeera, 23 October 2009.
24. Chris Kraul, 'Colombia Rebel Groups Recruiting Indigenous Youths', *Los Angeles Times*, 7 October 2009.
25. Ibid.
26. Trinidad, interview with author.
27. 'You'll Learn Not to Cry', Human Rights Watch.
28. Raúl Reyes, interview with author, Putumayo, Colombia, June 2007.
29. 'You'll Learn Not to Cry'Human Rights Watch.
30. Ingunn Bjørkhaug, 'Child Soldiers in Colombia: The Recruitment of Children into Non-State Violent Armed Groups', Microcon, June 2010.
31. Ibid.
32. 'You'll Learn Not to Cry', Human Rights Watch.
33. Horst Fischer, 'Collateral Damage', in Roy Gutman and David Rieff, *Crimes of War: What the Public Should Know* (New York: W.W. Norton, 1999), p. 88.
34. 'Landmine Monitor Report 2009: Toward and Mine-Free World', Landmine and Cluster Munition Monitor, 12 November 2009.
35. Ibid.
36. Diana Roa, interview with author, Bogotá, Colombia, 7 March 2002.
37. Reyes, interview with author.
38. 'Colombia: More FARC Killings with Gas Cylinder Bombs', Human Rights Watch, 15 April 2005.
39. Manuel Corrales, interview with author, Bellavista, Chocó, Colombia, 26 June 2003.
40. Ibid.
41. Jeremy McDermott, 'UN Condemns Colombia Massacre as War Crime', *The Scotsman*, 7 May 2002.
42. Corrales, interview with author.
43. Ibid.
44. Mario A. Murillo, *Colombia and the United States: War, Unrest and Destabilization* (New York: Seven Stories Press, 2004), p. 74.
45. McDermott, 'UN Condemns Colombia Massacre as War Crime'.

46. Winifred Tate, *Counting the Dead: The Culture and Politics of Human Rights Activism in Colombia* (Berkeley, CA: University of California Press, 2007), p. 288.

47. Adam Isacson, 'CINEP: Colombia's Conflict Is Far from Over', Center for International Policy, 10 April 2008. For an excellent report on military-paramilitary collusion during this period, see Human Rights Watch, *The 'Sixth Division': Military-Paramilitary Ties and U.S. Policy in Colombia* (New York: Human Rights Watch, 2001).

48. 'Estadisticas secuestro a 2006', Fundación País Libre, 2007.

49. Isacson, 'CINEP: Colombia's Conflict Is Far from Over'.

50. 'Paramilitary Demobilization', US Office on Colombia, 15 December 2007.

51. 'Colombia's New Armed Groups', International Crisis Group, 10 May 2007.

52. Alirio Uribe, interview with author, Riohacha, La Guajira, Colombia, 9 August 2006.

53. Isacson, 'CINEP: Colombia's Conflict Is Far from Over'. Note: The percentage of violations committed by the paramilitaries (29 per cent), military (56 per cent) and the FARC (10 per cent) do not total 100 per cent because the ELN and other small rebel groups were responsible for 5 per cent in 2006.

54. Review of the online archive of the *New York Times* conducted by the author in April 2007.

55. 'Colombia 2002–2006: Situación de derechos humanos y derechos humanitario', Comisión Colombiana de Juristas, January 2007.

56. Stanley J. Baran and Dennis K. Davis, *Mass Communication Theory: Foundations, Ferment, and Future* (Boston, MA: Wadsworth Cengage Learning, 2009), p. 293.

57. Kevin Whitelaw, "Inside Colombia's War on Kidnapping," *US News and World Report*, 27 February 2008.

58. 'Departamentos de llegada, años 2006–2007', Consultoría para los Derechos Humanos y el Desplazamiento (CODHES), 13 February 2008.

59. Tate, *Counting the Dead*, p. 163.

60. Ibid.

61. Ibid.

62. *World Report 2000*.

63. *World Report 2005*, Human Rights Watch, January 2005.

64. *World Report 2006*, Human Rights Watch, January 2006.

65. *World Report 2009*, Human Rights Watch, February 2009.

66. Tate, *Counting the Dead*, p. 166.

CHAPTER 7

1. Tim Padgett, 'Colombia's Stunning Hostage Rescue', *Time* magazine, 2 July 2008.

2. Alexander Biro Vare, interview with author, Inírida, Guainía, Colombia, 9 December 2010.

3. León Valencia, 'Las cifras del conflict en el 2010', *El Tiempo*, 8 December 2010.

4. Ibid.

5. 'Ending Colombia's FARC Conflict: Dealing the Right Card', International Crisis Group, 26 March 2009.

6. Isabel Coello, 'El gobierno Uribe es el que más personas ha desplazado', *Público*, 8 August 2010.

7. 'Colombia: Few Reasons for Optimism', Norwegian Refugee Council, 28 March 2008.

8. Jeremy McDermott, 'Alvaro Uribe Casts Long Shadow over Colombia Election', BBC News, 25 May 2010.

9. Adam Isacson, 'Para-Politics on the Ropes', Center for International Policy, 20 August 2008.

10. Colombia Monitor, 'Colombia Cracks Down', Washington Office on Latin America, July 2002.

11. Matt Apuzzo, 'Chiquita Pleads Guilty in Terror Probe', Associated Press, 19 March 2007.

12. James M. Dorsey, 'EU Lawmakers Urge Probe of Colombian Intelligence Operations', Deutsche Welle, 18 July 2010.

13. Adam Isacson, 'The New DAS Scandal', Center for International Policy, 27 February 2009.

14. *Human Development Report 2002*, United Nations Development Programme, 2002.

15. *Human Development Report 2009*, United Nations Development Programme, 2009.

16. Adam Isacson, 'Colombia: Don't Call It a Model', Washington Office on Latin America, July 2010.

17. Gustavo Petro, interview with author, Bogotá, Colombia, 15 June 2007.

18. Raúl Reyes, interview with author, Putumayo, Colombia, June 2007.

19. Steven Dudley, *Walking Ghosts: Murder and Guerrilla Politics in Colombia* (New York: Routledge, 2006), pp. 202–3.

20. Andrew Cawthorne, 'Chávez Urges Colombian Rebels to Put Down Arms', Reuters, 8 August 2010.

21. Jon, interview with author, Ibagué, Tolima, Colombia, 15 December 2010.

22. Luís Fernando Martinez, interview with author, Ibagué, Tolima, Colombia, 15 December 2010.

23. Nadja Drost, 'In Medellín, A Disturbing Comeback of Crime', *Time* magazine, 25 February 2010.

24. At the time of writing, Colombia's Constitutional Court had ruled that the base agreement was unconstitutional because it had not been approved by Colombia's Congress. It is not clear if the Colombian government will present the agreement to Congress for approval. Regardless of whether or

not the base agreement is ratified, the US government's desire to sign it illustrates the geopolitical importance of Colombia to the United States.

25. 'Military Construction Program: Fiscal Year (FY) 2010 Budget Estimates', US Air Force, May 2009.

26. Hugh O'Shaughnessy and Sue Bradford, *Chemical Warfare in Colombia: The Costs of Coca Fumigation* (London: Latin America Bureau, 2005), p. 26.

27. Tom Hennigan, 'FARC Talks Offer Sees New Colombian President Extend Olive Branch', *Irish Times*, 2 August 2010.

28. Reyes, interview with author.

29. Lieutenant-Colonel Rodolfo Mantilla, interview with author, Chaparral, Tolima, Colombia, 14 December 2010.

Bibliography

Allison, E., and R. Goldman (1999) 'Belligerent Status', in R. Gutman and D. Rieff (eds), *Crimes of War: What the Public Should Know*, New York: W.W. Norton.

Amnesty International (2003) 'Colombia: Trade Unionists and Human Rights Defenders Under Attack', August.

Amnesty International (2003) 'Possible Disappearance: Colombia Indigenous and Peasant Farmer Communities in Tame Municipality, Department of Arauca', June.

Amnesty International (2004) 'A Laboratory of War: Repression and Violence in Arauca', April.

Amnesty International (2004) *Amnesty International Report 2004*, May.

Amnesty International (2009) 'The Peace Community of San José de Apartadó: Communities in Resistance in Colombia', March.

Baran, S.J., and D.K. Davis (2009) *Mass Communication Theory: Foundations, Ferment, and Future*, Boston, MA: Wadsworth Cengage Learning.

Bjørkhaug, I. (2010) 'Child Soldiers in Colombia: The Recruitment of Children into Non-State Violent Armed Groups', Microcon, June.

Brittain, J.J. (2008) 'The Continuity of FARC–EP Resistance in Colombia', *Counterpunch*, August.

—— (2010) *Revolutionary Social Change in Colombia: The Origin and Direction of the FARC–EP*, London: Pluto Press

Bush, G.H.W. (1989) 'Statement on Trade Initiatives for the Andean Region', George Bush Presidential Library and Museum, November.

Center for International Policy (2003) 'Supplemental Aid for 2002', August.

Central Intelligence Agency (2005) 'Senior Executive Intelligence Brief', National Security Archive, Washington, DC, October.

Chernik, M. (1998) 'The Paramilitarization of the War in Colombia', *NACLA Report on the Americas*, March/April.

Chomsky, N. (2003) *Power and Terror: Post-9/11 Talks and Interviews*, New York: Seven Stories Press.

Clawson, P. L., and R.W. Lee III (1998) *The Andean Cocaine Industry*, New York: St. Martin's Press.

Colombian Ministry of Defence (2003) 'The Effectiveness of the Colombian Democratic Security and Defence Policy', August.

Comisión Colombiana de Juristas (2003) 'Alerta frente a las cifras gobernamentales sobre derechos humanos en Colombia', July.

—— (2004) 'Colombia: En contravía de las recomendaciones internacionales sobre derechos humanos, Balance de la política de seguridad democrática y la situación de derechos humanos y derecho humanitario, agosto 2002 a agosto 2004', October.

—— (2007) 'Colombia 2002-2006: Situación de derechos humanos y derechos humanitario', January.

Commission for the Study of Violence (1992) 'Organized Violence', in C. Bergquist, R. Peñaranda and G. Sánchez (eds), *Violence in Colombia: The Contemporary Crisis in Historical Perspective*, Wilmington, DE: Scholarly Resources.

Consultoría para los Derechos Humanos y el Desplazamiento (2008) 'Departamentos de llegada, años 2006-2007', February.

Crandall, R. (2002) *Driven by Drugs: U.S. Policy Toward Colombia*, Boulder, CO: Lynne Rienner.

Drexler, R.W. (1997) *Colombia and the United States: Narcotics Traffic and a Failed Foreign Policy*, Jefferson, NC: McFarland.

Fischer, H. (1999) 'Collateral Damage', in R. Gutman and D. Rieff (eds), *Crimes of War: What the Public Should Know*, New York: W.W. Norton.

Fundación País Libre (2007) 'Estadisticas secuestro a 2006', Bogotá, Colombia; accessed 27 August 2010.

Gibbs, T. (2007) Interview with Gladys Marín, June.

—— (2007) Interview with Miriam Narváez, June.

—— (2011) 'Voices from the Colombian Left: Women and the Struggle for Social Transformation', *Labour, Capital and Class*, forthcoming.

Graham, B. (2001) 'Excerpt from press conference with Sen. Bob Graham (D-Florida)', Center for International Policy, Washington, DC, October.

Guevara, E. (1995) *The Motorcycle Diaries: A Journey around South America*, London: Verso.

Hill, J. (2003) 'Regarding U.S. Narcotics Policy in Colombia', Senate Caucus on International Narcotics Control, US Senate, June.

Human Rights Watch (1996) *Colombia's Killer Networks: The Military–Paramilitary Partnership and the United States*, New York: Human Rights Watch

—— (1999) *World Report 2000*, December.

—— (2005) 'Colombia: More FARC Killings with Gas Cylinder Bombs', April.

—— (2001) *The 'Sixth Division': Military-Paramilitary Ties and U.S. Policy in Colombia*, New York: Human Rights Watch.

—— (2003) 'You'll Learn Not to Cry: Child Combatants in Colombia', September.

—— (2005) *World Report 2005*, January.

—— (2006) *World Report 2006*, January.

—— (2009) *World Report 2009*, February.

Hylton, F. (2006) *Evil Hour in Colombia*, London: Verso.

International Crisis Group (2007) 'Colombia's New Armed Groups', May.

International Trade Union Confederation (2009) 'Annual Survey of Violations of Trade Union Rights 2009', June.

Isacson, A. (2008) 'CINEP: Colombia's Conflict Is Far from Over', Center for International Policy, Washington, DC, April.

—— (2008) 'Para-Politics on the Ropes', Center for International Policy, Washington, DC, August.

—— (2009) 'The New DAS Scandal', Center for International Policy, February.

—— (2010) 'Colombia: Don't Call It a Model', Washington Office on Latin America, July.

Kamman, C.W. (2005) 'Paramilitaries Massacre as Many as 50 in Norte de Santander', National Security Archive, Washington, DC, October.

Keen, B. (1996) *A History of Latin America*, Boston, MA: Houghton Mifflin.

Leech, G. (2008) 'Bloody Foundation for U.S.–Colombia Free Trade Agreement', *Beacon Broadside*, April.

LeGrand, C. (1992) 'Agrarian Antecedents of the Violence', in C. Bergquist, R. Peñaranda and G. Sánchez (eds), *Violence in Colombia: The Contemporary Crisis in Historical Perspective*, Wilmington, DE: Scholarly Resources.

Logan, S. (2008) 'FARC's Revolution is Over', International Relations and Security Network, July.

Maddaloni, J. (2009) 'An Analysis of the FARC in Colombia: Breaking the Frame of FM 3–24', US Army School of Advanced Military Studies, Fort Leavenworth, KS.

Marshall, D. (1997) 'DEA Congressional Testimony', Subcommittee on National Security, International Affairs and Criminal Justice, July.

Marulanda Vélez, M. (2003) 'The Origins of the FARC–EP: The Birth of Armed Resistance', in R. Toledo, T. Gutierrez, S. Flounders and A. McInerny (eds), *War in Colombia: Made in U.S.A*, New York: International Action Center.

Molano, A. (1992) 'Violence and Land Colonization', in C. Bergquist, R. Peñaranda and G. Sánchez (eds), *Violence in Colombia: The Contemporary Crisis in Historical Perspective*, Wilmington, DE: Scholarly Resources.

—— (2000) 'The Evolution of the FARC: A Guerrilla Group's Long History', *NACLA Report on the Americas*, September/October.

Murillo, M.A. (2004) *Colombia and the United States: War, Unrest and Destabilization*, New York: Seven Stories Press.

NACLA Report on the Americas, (1998) 'Multilateral Invasion Force for Colombia?', May/June.

Norwegian Refugee Council (2008) 'Colombia: Few Reasons for Optimism', Oslo, March.

Organization of American States (2000) 'Annual Report of the Inter-American Commission on Human Rights 1999', April.

O'Shaughnessy, H., and S. Bradford (2005) *Chemical Warfare in Colombia: The Costs of Coca Fumigation*, London: Latin America Bureau.

Palacios, M. (2006) *Between Legitimacy and Violence: A History of Colombia, 1875–2002*, Durham, NC: Duke University Press.

Pizarro, E. (1992) 'Revolutionary Guerrilla Groups in Colombia', in C. Bergquist, R. Peñaranda and G. Sánchez (eds), *Violence in Colombia: The Contemporary Crisis in Historical Perspective*, Wilmington, DE: Scholarly Resources.

Plataforma Colombiana de Derechos Humanos, Democracia y Desarollo (2003) 'El Embrujo Autoritario: Primer Año de Gobierno de Álvaro Uribe Vélez', September.

Powell, C. (2001) 'Testimony on the International Campaign Against Terrorism', Senate Foreign Relations Committee, US Senate, October.

—— (2002) 'Press Conference from Bogotá', US Department of State, December.

—— (2003) 'Remarks After Meeting with Colombian President Alvaro Uribe', US Department of State, September.

Ramírez Cuellar, F. (2005) *The Profits of Extermination: How U.S. Corporate Power is Destroying Colombia*, Monroe, ME: Common Courage Press.

Rempe, D.M. (1995) 'Guerrillas, Bandits, and Independent Republics: US Counter-Insurgency Efforts in Colombia, 1959–1965', *Small Wars and Insurgencies*, Winter.

Revolutionary Armed Forces of Colombia – People's Army (FARC–EP) (1999) *FARC–EP: Historical Outline*, Toronto: International Commission, Revolutionary Armed Forces of Colombia – People's Army.

Richani, N. (2002) *Systems of Violence: The Political Economy of War and Peace in Colombia*, Albany, NY: State University of New York Press.

Ruiz, B. (2001) *The Colombian Civil War*, Jefferson, NC: McFarland.

Safford, F., and M. Palacios (2002) *Colombia: Fragmented Land, Divided Society*, New York: Oxford University Press.

Sánchez, G. (1992) 'The Violence: An Interpretive Synthesis', in C. Bergquist, R. Peñaranda and G. Sánchez (eds), *Violence in Colombia: The Contemporary Crisis in Historical Perspective*, Wilmington, DE: Scholarly Resources.

Sanders, J.E. (2004) *Contentious Republicans: Popular Politics, Race, and Class in Nineteenth-Century Colombia*, Durham, NC: Duke University Press.

Scott, P.D. (2003) *Drugs, Oil and War: The United States in Afghanistan, Colombia and Indochina*, Lanham, MA: Rowman & Littlefield.

Stokes, D. (2005) *America's Other War: Terrorizing Colombia*, London: Zed Books.

Tate, W. (1999) 'Colombia's Role in International Drug Industry', *Foreign Policy in Focus*, November.

—— (2007) *Counting the Dead: The Culture and Politics of Human Rights Activism in Colombia*, Berkeley, CA: University of California Press.

Taylor, F.X. (2001) 'Testimony of Francis X. Taylor, Coordinator of Counterterrorism',

House Committee on International Relations, US House of Representatives, October.

Thoumi, F.E. (2003) *Illegal Drugs, Economy, and Society in the Andes*, Baltimore: Johns Hopkins University Press.

Torres, C. (1969) 'Violence and Socio-Cultural Change in Rural Colombia', in M. Zeitlin (ed.), *Father Camilo Torres: Revolutionary Writings*, New York: Harper Colophon Books.

United Nations Development Programme (2002) *Human Development Report 2002*, New York: UNDP.

—— (2009) *Human Development Report 2009*, New York: UNDP.

Uribe, A. (2003) 'Palabras del Presidente Uribe en posesión de nuevo comandante de la FAC', Presidencia de la Republica, Bogotá, Colombia, September.

—— (2003) 'Discurso del Presidente Uribe en la Asamblea de Naciones Unidas', Presidencia de la Republica, Bogotá, Colombia, September.

US Air Force (2009) 'Military Construction Program: Fiscal Year (FY) 2010 Budget Estimates', Washington, DC, May.

US Department of Defense (2005) 'FARC Guerrilla Commanders and Paramilitary Group Members Comment on Their Organizations and Activities', National Security Archive, Washington, DC, October.

US Department of State (2000) 'Country Report on Human Rights Practices 1999', Washington, DC, February.

—— (2000) 'Fact Sheet: Colombia, U.N. Discussing Anti Coca Mycoherbicide Cooperation', Washington, DC, July.

—— (2001) 'Patterns of Global Terrorism 2000', Washington, DC, April.

—— (2010) 'Country Reports on Terrorism 2009', Washington, DC, August.

US Drug Enforcement Administration (2006) 'FARC Fact Sheet', Washington, DC, March.

—— (2006) 'United States Charges 50 Leaders of Narco-Terrorist FARC in Colombia with Supplying More than Half of the World's Cocaine', Washington, DC, March.

US Office on Colombia (2007) 'Paramilitary Demobilization', Washington, DC, December.

Vaicius, I., and A. Isacson (2003) 'The "War on Drugs" meets the "War on Terror"', Center for International Policy, Washington, DC, February.

Vargas Meza, R. (1998) 'The FARC, the War, and the Crisis of State', *NACLA Report on the Americas*, March/April.

Villalón, C. (2004) 'Cocaine Country', *National Geographic*, July.

Washington Office on Latin America (2003) 'Protecting the Pipeline: The US Military Mission Expands', Washington, DC, May.

Witness for Peace (2002) 'The Real Costs of Pipeline Protection in Arauca: Corporate Welfare with Deadly Consequences', July.

World Bank Group (2002) 'Colombia Poverty Report', March.

Wolf, P. (2007) 'Autopsy of a Narco-Guerrillera', WW4 Report, Washington, DC, March.

—— (2008) 'FARC Is Not a Terrorist Group', *Colombia Journal*, January.

Index